BIG TENCH

BIG TENCH

Edited by Bob Church

Contributors: Jim Gibbinson, Keith Sanders, Peter Jackson and Dave Harman

The Crowood Press

First published in 2005 by
The Crowood Press Ltd
Ramsbury, Marlborough
Wiltshire SN8 2HR

www.crowood.com

British Library Cataloguing-in-Publication Data
A catalogue record for this book is available from the British
Library.

ISBN 1 86126 814 9

Dedication
To the memory of Richard (Dick) Walker who inspired Bob
Church and many others to go on the 'big fish trail'.

Typeset by Jean Cussons Typesetting, Diss, Norfolk
Printed and bound in Great Britain by CPI Bath

Contents

Paul Thompson with an 8lb-plus fish from Sywell reservoir.

Foreword

I started fishing when I was six years old, but it wasn't until I was eleven that I caught my first tench from a small pond in Gerrards Cross. At 3lb it was about 2lb bigger than anything I had caught before, and tench have been a firm favourite ever since! As well as fishing I also read as much as I can about fishing. As I write this I can look around the room and see over 200 different angling titles. Amongst this collection I have, as far as I can tell, almost every tench angling book that has so far been printed, which I think at the moment is eighteen titles.

Quite a few of the titles mention the Tenchfishers group, which celebrated its fiftieth anniversary in 2004. I have been a member now since 1993 – in fact I became secretary and chairman only a few weeks after joining! But things have changed since then: from only eighteen members when I joined, and with a lot of help from the committee, the group now has over 150 members who exchange views and ideas, and I would suggest to anyone who wants to improve their tench fishing that they should join up. Details can be found on the website: www.tenchfishers.net

What can be said about the authors within these pages? If they are not angling legends already, they will be one day: Jim Gibbinson, inventor of the line aligner; Pete Jackson who, along with his wife Janet, has been catching tench for years; Keith Sanders, float angler extraordinaire; Dave Harman, one of the new breed of tench anglers and a Drennan Cup winner; and Bob Church who, with Pete and Janet Jackson, was one of the first to use a swimfeeder on Sywell reservoir, with devastating results – also now a good friend, I am proud to say.

Now that the tench 'season' has been lengthened by scrapping the old 'closed season', tench weights are on the increase and more anglers are fishing for tench, and this can only improve tench fishing.

With these authors each explaining their own special tactics for locating and catching some huge tench, the reader of this book will, undoubtedly, improve their own tench-fishing skills. I think that this book will become a 'must have' for any serious tench angler.

Paul Thompson
Tenchfishers Vice Chairman,
February 2005

Acknowledgements

I know that in my co-contributors I have selected a perfect balance, and I want to thank all four of them – Jim Gibbinson, Peter Jackson, Keith Sanders and Dave Harman – for doing an excellent job. This is the second in our series of single-species fishing books. I would also like to thank Bob Neville of Crowood Press, who always looks over my ideas with good support. Also thanks to Paul Thompson for his foreword; it makes a change for a young angler to write an overview like this. Finally I would like to thank Kay Church, my daughter-in-law, for typing my chapter.

1 Tench, an Early Love

by Bob Church

Tench were the very first species I fished for seriously, with specimen fish in mind. My first book was even called *Catch more Tench*, written for Wolfe Publishing back in 1974. I have always loved tench fishing: a dawn start, the early mist on the water, and then the telltale clusters of little bubbles that signal a feeding tench in your swim – and so the action would begin.

I have seen many tench-fishing dawns, sitting at the ready for that first bite. Of course if it was in the early season, from 16 June, I could expect a very big catch of possibly 100lb or more, on some occasions. Tench are bold biters early in the season, but they soon become wiser.

Having been put on record as the world's worst time-keeper, it never ceases

First view of the dam at Sywell when you walk from the car park.

9

1973: Bob with Pete Chillingworth, with a fine mixed catch of tench and big rudd. Bob's catch went 148½lb that day, filming for Angling Today *series of fishing programmes, with presenter Terry Thomas of ATV.*

to amaze my family and friends that I can be up and away by 3am for a first light, 4am tench-fishing session at nearby Sywell Reservoir. However, before I go on about my tench-fishing exploits, let me tell you briefly about my chosen four contributors.

MY CHOSEN CONTRIBUTORS

First there is Jim Gibbinson, a retired school teacher, my friend since the mid-sixties when he lived at Northampton, a fine angler for many species, and an out-standing writer; and when it comes to instruction, he's the best. He will cover the prolific gravel-pit tench fisheries.

One of the first characters from the Tenchfishers group with whom I formed a friendship is Peter Jackson. We met at Sywell after he tracked down myself and Rod Kilsby, following our capture of three 6lb-plus tench in 1966; at the time a 6lb tench was a monster, making headlines in the *Angling Times*. The British record for tench from 1950 to 1963 was as little as 8.5lb from a Leicester canal. However, like most other species, we have seen a massive increase in the average weights of tench at most waters. This trend I am told began in the late 1960s, when more and more nitrates and suchlike were being sprayed on the land by farmers, and which were eventually washed into our lakes. Once in the water, they fertilized the whole food chain therein, and together with today's global warming and high protein baits, it helps explain why it is now possible to catch tench of 10lb or more. However, I digress; but rest assured that Pete has fished for tench now for over fifty years, and you will enjoy reading and learning from his exploits.

And so to Keith Sanders: only if you are a very good tench fisher, or a passionate lover of float fishing for tench, will you have heard of Keith. But I tell you now, he is the best float fisher that I, and many other experts, have ever seen. He uses the most sensitive float systems, and gets bites that no one else would get, purely by his methods. You will all get so much from his chapter. Keith is now retired, and although not in the best of health, you will often see him on the dam wall at either Sywell or Hollowell reservoirs, where he has caught double-figure tench on the float from both waters. Keith is a life member of both the Northampton Specimen Group and the Tenchfishers.

Lastly there is the man the *Angling Times* called 'Mr Tench Fisher': Dave Harman. Up until 2004 he has caught seventeen double-figure tench, and importantly, these have come from five different waters: an amazing angling feat. You will learn how to catch the largest tench after studying his chapter!

A CLOSE SEASON FOR TENCH?

Although I am a strong believer in keeping a river close season, especially as far as barbel are concerned, my views change for tench. For example, the tench at Sywell usually spawn on 9 July precisely, three weeks after the opening of the close season, and this makes a complete mockery of keeping the close season for tench at Sywell, and elsewhere in stillwaters, because some of the best fishing time is then lost.

I suggest the various riparian owners should look again at the close season for tench on any stillwater, because they nearly always spawn in the open season after 16 June. They also go into a sort of non-feeding, non-biting mood for at least a month afterwards. For these reasons, the present close season for tench is way out, and because of the unproductive fishing that follows, there should be no close season for tench in stillwaters.

SUMMER FISHING IN THE SIXTIES

Perhaps the thing I like most about tench fishing is the successful method used by Rod Kilsby and myself in the mid-sixties, one that still works as well as any other method today. I refer, of course, to open-end swim-feeder ledgering. I proved this a couple of seasons back whilst catching a few tench at Sywell for Sky television, when in Keith Arthur's programme *Tight Lines* I was able to demonstrate just how the old swim-feeder could beat the more modern boilies and suchlike.

Tackle

Here is my tackle set-up. I fish with two rods of 12ft in length, the 1.5lb test-curve Bob Church/Tony Gibson multi-specialist rod, the very same with which Tony caught the record first-ever 20lb barbel. I use

Bob Church with his first six-pounder from Sywell in 1966.

Shimano Bait-runner 5000 RE reels loaded with 6lb or 8lb new Kryston line, a fairly low-diameter, top-grade copolymer with a fluorocarbon coating; it enables me to cast long distances with effortless ease, and it has great knot strength. It is also clear and becomes invisible under water.

Nowadays I get even more bites if I use a 4lb hook-length, and for this I use around 15in of Ashima clear fluorocarbon with a no. 10 swivel at one end, and my size 12, Super Specialist Drennan hook at the other. The actual open-end feeders are best made from clear plastic.

Bait

Bait consists of maggots of yellow, white or red, so I buy half a gallon of mixed. Then I experiment with sandwich-bait set-ups.

Tackle and dough-bobbin bite indicators from the mid-sixties. I often still use the latter even today.

This can be simply three white maggots and a tiny pinch of white breadflake on the hook shank; or stick the point of the hook in the centre of the rear end of a big maggot, and then push it so it travels round the hook bend and stops at the eye. This hides the hook shank completely. Now put just two more maggots on the hook (I favour red): nick them only just through the skin, one on at the rear end and the other at the pointed end; this stops spin when casting and retrieving. When you look at the presentation you will see what I mean, in that you cannot see any hook at all. A tiny pinch of breadflake is squeezed on near the hook eye, and at times this can make all the difference between success and failure.

Dragging

A method that includes dragging is in fact very little different to how I fished way back in the mid-sixties at Sywell. In

Bob would always drag a swim out, then bait up pre-season.

13

TENCH, AN EARLY LOVE

September 1968 I wrote an article in the old *Fishing* magazine: here is what I said at the time:

On some tench waters to drag is strictly taboo. On Sywell however, a thorough dragging is a definite 'must' – it is, in fact, the most important factor between success and failure. Great barriers of soft, long-stemmed weeds grow far out into the lake, and to clear some of these – usually a 4yd to 5yd wide channel, going out a distance of 25yd to 30yd – usually means a good catch – say, 100lb – the following morning during the early season.

The second morning after dragging the catch will drop, and it continues to do so until the swim is dragged again, or a new swim is prepared, when the numbers of fish will once more increase. At one stage

100lb bags of tench were common on opening day, 16 June. Here Peter Jackson shows his big catch at Sywell in 1967.

When you do the dragging and baiting, a catch like this will be yours: Bob's son Stephen displays the morning catch.

this year, when the fishing began to get difficult, I cleared a new swim some 100yd from our 'hot-spot' area. I fished there on the following morning, and between 7am and 9am I caught six nice fish to 5lb 2oz. Had I not dragged, I would most certainly have failed, as did most other anglers fishing the water that morning.

The aquatic insect life of the lake is remarkably diverse, and I would like to be able to identify the numerous varieties we have discovered while dragging. There have been some really strange ones among

Bob and Pete Jackson meet up at Sywell. Pete helps Bob return a big catch at dusk. The 1967 results of swim-feeder ledgering.

them, as well as all the common and expected species. The fish undoubtedly feed on these small food items, and this is almost certainly the reason for the great success of maggot as bait: we have tried other baits, but none can compare with the mighty maggot. Although the water holds swan mussel in plenty, the tench won't look at them when they are used as bait.

Swim-feeder ledgering has been the successful method used by Rod Kilsby (a fellow member of the Northampton Specimen Group) and myself. We know all about the arguments regarding the crudeness of this method, but we are interested only in catching tench, and we catch far more when we use swim-feeders than by any other method. This includes swan-shot link-ledgering, although Peter Jackson has done well when using a swan-shot link and groundbait cupping. When using two rods I have experimented with a swim-feeder on one, and a link-ledger and groundbait cupping on the other, and the results have been strongly in favour of the swim-feeder: for example, five fish to one, and four to nil, each in a morning session.

My swim-feeder is packed with a half-inch of brown-crumb groundbait at one end, then filled up well with loose maggots, and finally packed tightly again with groundbait at the other end. Pinpoint casting will groundbait these maggots about thirty yards out in the lake. Then if I haven't had a bite after the swim-feeder has been out about five minutes, I remove my dough-bobbin, wind in the slack, pull in a couple of feet of slack line, and replace the bobbin.

This is usually the best time for a bite. What happens is this: I move the swim-feeder sharply, which deposits the maggots as the container moves forwards. This brings my maggot hookbait into the area where all the maggots are, and sometimes I have had tugs while I have been actually moving the bait; in fact, one fish of more than 5lb was taken in this manner, as well as several others.

There are two widely held beliefs about tench fishing: that sun-up followed by clear skies and bright sun means no more fish; and that not much sport follows a falling water temperature – but these two have been completely disproved. In fact, we have felt that the tench have been even keener on bright mornings; and while the water temperature dropped from 67° to 62° in a few days, three 6lb fish and some of 5lb-plus were taken.

Rod Kilsby caught two of the six-pounders, and in doing so performed one of angling's rare achievements: he landed a six-pounder, unhooked it and put it in the keep net, and with the very next cast had an even better fish of 6.4lb. We had then taken four 6lb fish from one swim in twelve months, plus several of 5lb plus.

The sun was up high at mid-day, and Bob gets a perfect tench of 8lb 6oz from the West Arm.

Watching catches generally, it was noticeable that some swims were producing bigger fish than others, and one had the impression that margin-patrolling shoals were moving in set areas. One other swim that was producing good fish was being worked over by two friends, Bob Tate and Dave Boothroyd, who captured nine 5lb-plus fish in five days. Theirs was a very different swim to ours: it was chopped through a deep bed of rushes that ended in open water, and it was only necessary to cast where the rushes ended, or just beyond, to catch fish. This was a shallower swim than ours, and it was noticeable that it produced most fish when the water temperature was climbing to 67° and more.

Most of the fish below 4lb have been males, and these have averaged around 3.75lb. Fish of less than 3lb have been almost unheard of. Each of us now has an average of over 4lb. My personal best male went to 4lb 9 oz, and I also had two more of 4.5lb apiece, and several over 4lb. Peter's best male was 4lb 10oz. This was a very high average weight for males, and they can certainly fight! They really do go well. The female fish in this water, even before spawning, are a nice shape: good and thick with a high back. And no! unfortunately we have not seen any cruising around that could go into double figures, though we shall keep looking! Our next step is a seven-pounder, and I am sure this is well within the bounds of possibility.

We are not bothered too much by 'nuisance' fish. An occasional roach or perch is landed, or sometimes a 'muncher' has a crack at our swim-feeder on the retrieve. We have used line from 5lb to 6lb breaking strain, and have found this adequate so far. We also have great faith in small hooks, provided they are best quality and tied direct. I go smaller than most, using sizes 14 and 16.

So much for this summer's tenching

Bob with a good male fish of 6lb 5oz; it was one of the largest caught at the time – 1973.

(1968). Our plans are already going ahead for next, for we feel we can do even better! Of course the last thirty-seven years have shown we all have much better sport on many tench waters up and down the country.

TALKING BIG FISH

I had to recall this article of mine from the old but excellent (and now long gone) EMAP *Fishing* magazine. It clearly shows that the methods of today are not that different, but the size of the fish most surely is. In 1968, 5lb to 6lb fish were the best you could hope for, whereas now it is 7lb to 9lb, with the distinct possibility of a double. I am informed of a 12lb 4oz fish caught in September 2003, so Sywell is looking good for the future.

Talking of big fish, pound for pound, tench are known to be one of the better fighting coarse fish. Over the years I have regularly praised their fighting ability, but always noticed that it was the male fish that tested my tackle most of all. For the less experienced, the male tench is usually always smaller than the female, and can be easily identified because it has much larger, cup-shaped pelvic fins and thicker, lumpy fin roots. The female is a plumper, more rounded shape even after spawning.

Living so close to Sywell reservoir, I suppose I have been spoilt somewhat. My records show I have taken 100lb-plus bags from four other stillwaters as well as Sywell, so my knowledge of tench has a sound base. I had noticed how the male tench were getting larger at Sywell because for many years they had topped out at a maximum of around 5lb. I remember being pleased with a 5lb 5oz male, then the following year I had a great fight from a male of 6lb 10oz, and thought that perhaps this was the limit.

My Super Fish

Then in the 1992 season came my super fish. I had a 4am start fishing on the edge of the deep water some seventy-five yards from the left side of the dam wall. This was a favourite Sywell swim of mine and it held many good catch memories, but none that would compare to this day.

I had one bite during the session using an open-end swim-feeder as usual, and a sandwich hookbait of two maggots and a pinch of breadflake on a size 12 hook. Bites at Sywell are rarely missable, and this fish was now hooked on 6lb nylon and my ever-faithful Mitchell 400 reel. The fish hung deep, staying over the ledge, and I felt the nylon rubbing the bottom. I applied medium pressure and kept my rod well up, hoping to coax the fish into the shallower water. Instead it took off on a long run towards the middle, where it stopped for a few seconds, then went off again; it was now about eighty yards away.

I kept patient, knowing that too much pressure would do more harm than good and might result in losing the fish through the line breaking or the hook straightening. Slowly I brought it in, and with a final foam-swirling flurry at the net, he was mine: the largest male tench I had ever seen, at 7lb 6oz. Of course, that was thirteen years ago; nowadays the males are getting even larger, and the tackle has changed.

Dubious Fishing Practice

About ten years ago many visiting anglers began to use boilies, and these were soon successful, with plenty of big tench falling to them. However, controversy was soon to erupt, as some fishing practices were called into question. Longer-range fishing with breaking-strain lines of 12lb to 15lb, and heavy lead bolt rigs began to cause damage

A really big male at the time – 1992 – and I suppose it is still big even by today's standards: 7lb 6oz.

Bob's silhouette, and it produced an 8lb beauty!

Gavin Walding plays a good tench as the light fades.

Here, Gavin briefly poses for a photo: it's such a beauty, the yellow coloration is from a new batch of fast-growing fish at Sywell – the weight 8lb 2oz.

to the mouth of a lot of fish. Hooked tench were being reeled in from way out in the reservoir, and many would snag up in thick beds of soft weed and their lips and mouths were getting torn quite badly. Eventually it was considered a serious enough issue for the fishes' welfare to be put first, and the then controlling club – Wellingborough and District – had to ban all ledgering techniques.

I am pleased to say that after a few seasons this ban was reversed, and now light ledgering techniques with a bomb or feeder are permitted as long as they are used sensibly.

SYWELL IN MORE RECENT YEARS

Sywell has been at top water level all winter, and whenever this has happened in the

Dick Bateman fishes both Sywell and Hollowell reservoirs. This is Hollowell, and Dick proudly shows his 10lb 12oz tench, a fine-shaped fish.

past there is good fishing at the start of the season. The tench tend to come in closer during the first couple of hours of light: I have caught as many as ten fish just light float fishing two rod-lengths out while wading in the rushes. I could not fail, as the tell-tale feeding bubbles showed me exactly where to cast.

Keith Sanders maintains that although two rods *can* be fished, seemingly giving you twice as many chances, in fact it is absolute concentration on one light float rig that can in fact greatly increase the catch. This is far more noticeable once the early, easier fishing has passed. To prove the point, I asked Keith how many Sywell tench he now catches in a season: evidently in 1999 to 2000 he landed 350 tench, with the last one coming on the last day of the season, with his last cast. By comparison, this current year up to Christmas he has caught 369.

Dick Bateman, whom I know from the barbel scene, has taken some good catches from Sywell more recently; he uses float tactics most of the time. Just look at this for a catch one day in September 2002:

8.00am:	6lb 14oz male
9.30am:	7lb 2oz male
12.30pm:	6lb 8oz female
12.45pm:	8lb 2oz female
1.15pm:	7lb 2oz female
1.45pm:	6lb 12oz female
3.00pm:	6lb 10oz female
3.15pm:	7lb 3oz male
3.30pm:	7lb 6oz female
4.10pm:	7lb 9oz male
4.45pm:	5lb 0oz male
6.00pm:	6lb 4oz female
7.00pm:	6lb 8oz female

Dick is concentrating his attention on barbel these days, but he still gets up to Sywell for a few sessions on the new day-ticket system.

Another friend of mine from the barbel world is Paul Thompson, though of course he is very much involved with tench fishing as well, so we have plenty in common. Paul is a committee member of the national Tenchfishers club, and Sywell has always been a favourite amongst them, something that dates back to the mid-sixties and the Pete Jackson era.

Paul was fishing there last season, and in his opinion: 'Sywell is not as easy these days as many anglers think.' Of course on the right day everything goes well and you can expect an average four or six fish during each session; '…but on the wrong day it can be a right bitch, without a single bite coming.'

'Raking the swim was always a chore that worked for me,' said Paul; and his final tip was, 'Don't try to cast to the middle of the reservoir unless you are really desperate, and then cast with only one rod. You can catch fish from three rod-lengths out by sitting quiet.'

CATCHING THE SUPER SPECIMEN

To sum up, this book will help those quite experienced tench anglers learn more about how to catch the super specimens. We can all learn from Dave Harman, who has learnt how to catch the largest tench from so many different waters; Keith Sanders' float-fishing style will give you many more tench from now on, so study his techniques thoroughly; and again, we can all benefit from the wide experience of Jim Gibbinson and Pete Jackson. It's a great team.

Although I do admit to being somewhat old-fashioned where tench methods are concerned, this is not to say that I don't try

Bob took his pike-fishing mate Mike Green for a day's tench fishing at Sywell in 2004 – he soon hooked a big one.

Mike with his Sywell tench; at 7lb 14oz he was well pleased as it was a personal best.

several methods, even though I usually come back to the same open-ended swim-feeder tactics as pioneered by Rodney and myself in the early sixties. Why? Because this tactic still catches me most tench – ask Pete, he caught a seven-pounder when trying it out.

Four years before this book appeared the Tek-Neek fishing tackle company took over the lease at Sywell. But since that time, anglers' visits slumped, even though the good tench there were as plentiful as ever. To address this problem, the Tek-Neek chairman at the time, Bill Hutchison, slashed the price of a day ticket to £6, and made a full season permit £96 – excellent value, to my mind. A new regular bailiff was also installed.

There is also the now-annual tench-fishing national open competition, held for the first time at Sywell reservoir in early June 2005; fifty tickets are allocated and all quickly get sold, so apply early. Sywell is now a country park and spectators are welcome, so the prize-giving takes place at the visitors' buildings behind the dam wall in the afternoon. Again, it is Bill Hutchison who has made this day possible. The purpose of the competition is simple: to find out the potential at Sywell for size and numbers of tench. Is it still as good as it used to be? Will a double-figure tench come out on the day?

Most importantly, this is a great social day out for all tench-fishing entrants. I know from my catches at Sywell last year – 2004 – there is a new batch of young, fast-growing tench coming through. These are all yellowish in colour rather than the normal olive, but most interesting are their weights, which went from 8lb to 9.4lb. Now, is this new batch of super tench going to be doubles this year? By the time this book is published we shall all know...

2 Gravel Pit Tench

by Jim Gibbinson

Tench do well in gravel pits. They can usually maintain their numbers by natural recruitment, so there is no need to top up the population with stock fish – and importantly, given the subject of this book, they grow large. I'm not suggesting that gravel pits have the monopoly in this latter regard, but it's fair to say that they lead the field.

Although most anglers are aware that tench grow bigger than used to be the case, few realize just how dramatic the change has been. Perhaps I can best illustrate its magnitude by pointing out that prior to 1950 only two tench over 7lb had been recorded – and the weight of one of those was disputed! The captor, Mr B. S. Dawson, claimed the fish at a new record weight of 7lb 6oz, but doubts arose when the taxidermists, Messrs J. Cooper and Sons, said that when delivered to them it weighed, quote: '6lb 2oz with newspaper and in a frozen state' (*Angler's News*, 7 August 1948). I love the explanation offered by Mr Cooper for the discrepancy: 'I can only presume Mr Dawson weighed it on a spring balance which had strained a pound.' How's that for diplomacy! Notwithstanding the evidence of Messrs Cooper and Sons, and the controversy that raged in the leading angling periodicals of the time, the *Angler's News* and the *Fishing Gazette*, the fish was subsequently ratified as the record at the weight claimed by its captor.

Nowadays, a 7lb 6oz tench would hardly rate a mention in either *Angling Times* or *Angler's Mail*, unless it was caught in mid-January, in the middle of a blizzard, at the end of a slow newsweek!

Many anglers attribute to boilies the dramatic increase in tench size, but you don't have to look too deeply at this hypothesis to see that it does not withstand scrutiny. Chief among its shortcomings is the fact that big tench are not confined to waters that receive lots of boilies; indeed, they are often found in waters that hardly see a boilie from year's beginning to year's end.

Another widely held belief is that global warming has provided tench with a longer growing season, thereby enabling them to profit from the cumulative effect of extra weight-gain each year. If that were the case, we would see tench being active for longer; but examination of tench captures in the angling weeklies sees them fizzle out in September, just as they did previously. Furthermore, if temperature were the key, then surely shallow waters that warm up quickly and reach higher temperatures would produce bigger tench than deep waters. But do they? Not in my experience.

Another effect of global warming would be the extension of the tench's range northwards. But there's no evidence that this is happening, either.

So, if the answer lies neither with boilies nor global warming, why have we seen

Tench of this size are the results of eutrophication.

both the average size of tench, and the maximum size to which they grow, go inexorably up and up?

It is because our waters have become enriched with nutrients as a result of eutrophication, which in turn is the consequence of accumulations of nitrates and phosphates (primarily from farm fertilizer, detergents and sewage) in groundwater and, occasionally, surface run-off. Gravel pits, due to their direct connection with groundwater via seepage from the water table, get more than their share of this chemical input, which is why they are synonymous with big tench (and bream and carp, for that matter).

There is, as they say, no such thing as a free lunch, so there is a price to be paid for our tench growing as large as they do. First, and most obvious, eutrophic enrichment has resulted in many of our waters becoming very much weedier than hitherto. In the late seventies and early eighties I caught 7lb-plus tench from Johnson's Island and Road Lakes, and the adjacent Greensands Lake (near Maidstone, Kent), on small hooks and 4lb breaking-strain line. I was able to use such light tackle because the waters were virtually weed free. But by the late eighties the situation had changed markedly, and to stand a realistic chance of extracting fish from dense beds of *Elodea* and milfoil, it became necessary to use carp rods and at least 12lb line.

Worse, eutrophic waters are susceptible to algal blooms. When algae die, the dissolved oxygen content of the water may drop to a dangerously low level. Tench can cope with this situation better than most species, but even they might die if the problem persists. At the very least, fishing will be adversely affected due to the development of anoxic conditions close to the bottom. So there's the equation: big fish on the one hand, excessive weed and potentially dangerous algae on the other.

Another factor that has become relevant in recent years is cormorant predation. The elimination of North Sea herring stocks by commercial fishing fleets has forced cormorants to move inland to feed. If I were a roach specialist or a match angler I'd be tearing my hair out at the way cormorants have been allowed to plunder fish stocks in our rivers and lakes (though recent changes in legislation suggest that at long last the problem has been recognized and is being addressed), but as a big fish angler, I have to concede that they have, in a perverse way, been of benefit. Cormorants can cope with fish up to about 1.5lb in weight, with their preferred prey about half that size; the outcome of which is that untold millions of roach and rudd, along with immature specimens of larger species, have slipped down the throats of cormorants. This has resulted in the overall biomass of many waters being dramatically reduced, creating a situation whereby increased food supplies (as a result of the aforementioned eutrophication) are shared between fewer mouths.

So it's hardly any wonder that tench grow larger than previously, is it?

CREATION AND CATEGORIZATION

Before proceeding further, I would like to look in detail at gravel pits, for I believe that the more we know about the waters we fish, the more successful we are likely to be.

Gravel layers – or 'terraces', as they are called – were deposited by retreating ice-fronts or torrential meltwater in Pleistocene interglacial periods. In geological terms this occurred very recently – within the last 300,000 years. These gravel terraces provided the aggregates to supply an extensive and expanding post-war programme of construction and road building.

Where gravel excavations occurred in areas having a high water table, the resulting holes in the ground flooded and became lakes. The fact that these lakes had a direct link with the water table saved them from the ignominious fate of being used as landfill sites, because commercial, industrial and domestic waste contains pollutants, which in turn could have contaminated subterranean aquifers.

Gravel pits vary considerably in size. The smallest are cosy little ponds of less than an acre, and often lie alongside roads or railways where the aggregate was used for foundation bedding. The largest, by contrast, can be massive windswept expanses of eighty acres or more. They vary in depth, too. The oldest pits are invariably shallow – rarely deeper than ten feet – because only the aggregate affording easiest access was extracted. These first-generation pits, as I call them, are characterized by islands, submerged ridges (bars), flat-topped humps (plateaux), and mounds created by the dumping of unwanted topsoil and spoil.

Where bars exist, they usually run parallel – anything from five to twenty-five yards apart – with channels of deeper water between. This is a consequence of the method of aggregate removal used in older pits, whereby the excavators dug and dumped in a linear pattern. In some pits, however, a second line of excavation, at right angles to the first, was employed. This resulted in them having what is best described as an egg-box configuration.

Pits dug through the 1960s and early 1970s – which I refer to as second generation – tend to be somewhat deeper (averaging twelve to seventeen feet) due to the development of improved digging techniques, which made deeper excavation and the extraction of lower-grade aggregates economically viable.

While second-generation pits often have islands and shallow plateaus, they are generally devoid of bars because post-1960s legislation required that most of the spoil be used to backfill other pits in the vicinity.

Third-generation gravel pits – those dug since the late 1970s – are deeper still due to excavations going down to and sometimes below the greensand layer. They average fifteen to twenty-five feet, but sometimes exceed thirty feet. The deepest I have fished (Stonar Lake near Sandwich, Kent) has a maximum depth of over fifty feet.

A characteristic of third-generation pits is the presence of a particularly deep area, usually in a corner, the original purpose of which was to enable water to be drained away from the excavations via gullies, whereupon it was pumped into a nearby disused pit which had been exhausted of its aggregates.

Sometimes third-generation pits have islands and extensive shallows created by sediment produced by gravel washing. Initially such deposits are extremely soft – like quicksand in fact – but over the course of time the sediment consolidates and may become quite firm. These sedimentary areas are usually found in just one or two sections of the pit where they create large plateau-like expanses, but they can sometimes take the form of elongated promontories.

Very occasionally, third-generation pits have a gently sloping ramp going down into the water, the original function of which was to give lorries access to the floor of the pit. In truth, though, it's a rare feature of gravel pits, being more commonly associated with deep chalk pits.

In addition to varying in size and depth, gravel pits come in a wide variety of shapes. The oldest, due to extensive spoil dumping, tend to be irregular in form with lots of bays and points; newer pits are likely to be more or less rectangular.

Some second-generation pits are shaped roughly like an hourglass; this was the result of a pit being dug close to a previous excavation with just a few yards of earth wall between them, the purpose of which was to prevent water from the abandoned pit flooding the new one. When the new pit was completed, it too became abandoned and filled with water; over the course of time, winter storms battered and eroded the barrier, causing it to collapse, thereby allowing the two pits to become connected.

Another distinctive form is what I call the 'fat boomerang'. Examples of this type include the Carp Society's Horseshoe Lake near Lechlade, and the main lake at Suffolk Water Park near Ipswich. Their characteristic boomerang configuration is the result of partial backfilling with spoil.

MAPPING

Due to the features and depth variations likely to be encountered in a gravel pit, I think it is essential to undertake a survey to get a clear idea of what lies beneath the surface. The best way, without doubt, is to go out on the water with a boat and an echo sounder. If boats aren't allowed, a good alternative is a Smartcast portable echo sounder, designed specifically for bank use. This ingenious bit of kit has a small egg-shaped transducer that is tied to the end of the line and cast in the normal way. I've never used one, but my younger son Peter has, and he's a great fan. Its disadvantages are that it has limited range (about thirty yards), and it is confused by big waves. Oh yes, and pike will attack it as it is drawn across the surface! My friend Steve Burke, who controls the syndicate fisheries at Wingham, near Canterbury, had a Smartcast transducer grabbed several times in one day on the largest lake in the complex! Clearly, a wire or Quicksilver trace is a requirement in waters holding pike. The broad-spectrum picture obtained by means of an echo sounder can then be augmented by detailed swim-mapping from the bank with a conventional through-the-lead feature-finding outfit.

Contrived though it sounds, I was engaged in a preliminary swim-mapping exercise earlier today. The pit concerned is a 25–30 acre third-generation pit to which I have recently gained access. Boats are not allowed on the water, so I'm compelled to work from the bank. This morning I chose three swims on the east bank, which took my fancy due to their exposure to westerly and south-westerly winds. From each swim I made a series of fanned casts, and measured the depth every ten yards or so from approximately seventy yards out all the way back to the margins. I'll do the same for a number of other swims – a few on each bank – until I'm satisfied that I have the sort of broad-spectrum picture that, had boats been allowed, I would have obtained by means of an echo sounder. I will then identify those swims that strike me as being particularly interesting, whereupon I will undertake careful and very detailed plumbing, with distances accurately measured by means of a Shakespeare line counter.

I first came across this useful little gadget in an article by Shaun Harrison, whereupon I went straight out and bought one. They aren't expensive; at the time of writing mine cost about £12, if I remember correctly. For the benefit of those who have never seen one, I should explain that it's a matchbox-size device that is attached to the rod to enable boat anglers – notably when deep-water trolling – to measure how much line has been paid out. If, however, it is mounted on the rod the wrong way round – which is how Shaun described its use, and how I use it for swim mapping – it gives a precise measurement of how much line has been retrieved. My model is calibrated in feet, but a metric version is available for those who prefer to work in metres.

This reminds me that I should explain my somewhat schizoid attitude to imperial and metric measurement. I refer to rod lengths and water depths in feet, casting distances in yards, fish weights and line breaking-strains in pounds, and lead weights in ounces. For hook-links I use centimetres. Hair lengths (as in hair rigs) and boilie sizes I express in millimetres. Hectares are a mystery to me, so I describe water area in acres. With regard to temperature I have yet to decide, vacillating freely and with no apparent logic between Fahrenheit and Celsius! Like most people, I use what makes sense to me – who, for example, can make any sense of a '3.81m rod'? (It's 12ft 6in, by the way.)

Let us return to the subject in hand, swim-mapping, and at how a line counter is used to do this. First, it is clipped to the rod the wrong way round, as previously mentioned, and the tension adjuster turned to maximum. With the line detached from the counter, a through-the lead plumbing set-up is used to find features of interest: the edge of a slope, the base of a plateau, the nearside of a weedbed, a gap in a bar and suchlike. When an interesting feature is identified, the marker-float is lined up against something on the far bank such as a pylon or a dip in the tree line. The float is then wound down tight to the lead, and the line is engaged in the line counter (which is zeroed). The line is then retrieved through the counter until the end-tackle reaches the rod tip; at which point the distance is recorded in a notebook.

Let us suppose, for purposes of illustration, that the line counter tells me I have retrieved 105ft (35yd) of line. If, on a subsequent occasion, I want to place my baited tackle in that precise spot, I tether my terminal tackle somewhere behind my swim and pay out 105ft along the bank (again using the line counter, but this time the correct way round), and tie a brightly coloured pole-elastic line marker adjacent to my tip ring. Then I clip up (more of which later), and wind the line back on the reel. I am now ready to cast towards my far bank sight-marker, and providing my direction accuracy is good, my terminal rig will land in precisely the right spot.

No matter how frequently I need to recast that rod, I know that if I realign the pole-elastic with my tip ring, and then clip up, the terminal tackle will drop just right every time.

I've been teased, mocked even, about my obsession with accurate swim-mapping, but I regard it as an essential element in my fishing. Apart from the obvious benefit of having a detailed knowledge of the topography of my waters, it has the additional advantage that I can arrive at my swim and achieve accurate bait placement without first needing to plumb around with a feature-finding outfit, thereby avoiding potentially fish-scaring disturbance.

LOCATION

Having a detailed knowledge of the water

is only useful if we are able to interpret it – which brings us to the most important aspect of gravel-pit tench fishing: finding them.

In some waters tench readily reveal their whereabouts by rolling. I love seeing this because I've found that where they roll, they also feed. But rolling is rare in some waters, and even in those waters where it does occur, we can't rely on it happening; in which case, we have to look at what we know about the fish's behaviour and preferences, and try to work out where they might be.

Tench are generally regarded as being shallow-water fish. But while they group up in shallow areas for spawning – usually in the same spots each year – they drift off to deeper areas when spawning has finished. It is not, however, a mass movement such as we see with carp, but rather the gradual departure of individual females after they have shed their spawn. Furthermore the males don't follow immediately, but hang about until all the females have gone. This is why some swims produce more males than females until the first or second week in July, whereupon the swims die completely.

When spawning is over and done with, we shouldn't be frightened to fish deep water. I say that in the knowledge that the words 'tench' and 'shallow water' are inextricably linked in many anglers' minds, and they wouldn't fish what they considered to be deep water. But such reluctance is misplaced, because deep water is a perfectly normal habitat for tench. I would estimate that between half and three-quarters of my 7lb-plus fish have been caught in depths of twelve to fifteen feet, with a significant proportion coming from depths of fifteen to eighteen feet. And I've caught a few in water deeper than eighteen feet – not many, admittedly, but enough to know that such depths fall within their normal range.

The deepest water from which I've caught tench was twenty-one feet, but I'd be surprised if even that proved to be their lower limit.

Tench like weed – or to put it another way, they are often found in the vicinity of weed, whether for food or because it offers security, I'm not sure. I'm talking primarily of bottom weed such as milfoil and *Elodea*, but during early summer, surface and emergent plants such as *Potamogeton*, lilies and reeds also have an appeal.

They like areas of depth change, the most obvious of which is the margin slope, but the sides of islands, bars and humps are good, too. Most of my big tench have come from swims that incorporated a slope of one sort or another.

In second- and third-generation pits with substantial areas of deep water, the top of a plateau will almost certainly be a productive spot, even if the depth is only a couple of feet shallower than the surrounding area. In the case of a plateau that rises to within a few feet of the surface, I wouldn't confine my attention to its top, but would fish its sides, too.

The most reliable spots of all, though, are what I refer to as 'holding swims'. In most pits there are areas that are particularly favoured by tench; it's almost as if they live there – the tench equivalent of residential suburbia, in fact! How to find these places? As mentioned earlier, rolling can be a good clue as to their whereabouts, but often it is a matter of trying different swims until such a spot is found. Once located, a holding swim is likely to remain productive for weeks at a time, even if subjected to quite intense angling pressure. There are positive and negative aspects to this. On the plus side of the equation, it makes for reliable fishing – which is nice if the water is neglected and there is no competition for swims, because it means you can drop on the tench almost at will. The

A big male tench. Males aren't always pretty, but they fight like demons!

negative aspect is that productive swims don't remain vacant if the water is popular, and once you've demonstrated its potential you'll be lucky to get in it again! A further down side is that the poor tench get absolutely hammered because, unlike carp, they don't move away from angling pressure.

As an example of holding swims remaining productive over a sustained period, and also to illustrate the effects of wind on tench location, I would like to cite the example of Johnson's Railway Lake. When I fished there, there were two swims that, depending on the time of year, were almost 100 per cent reliable. One, which I called the 'Cubby Hole', was my first choice until mid-August. Only rarely was I thwarted in my attempts to secure the swim, because it was too tight to accommodate a bivvy, and thereby neglected by carp anglers.

I caught lots of big tench from the Cubby Hole, and even helped two anglers catch their first-ever seven-pounders by putting them in the swim with the instruction to 'Cast with a gentle underarm lob in the direction of that tall poplar.' Tenching by numbers, as it were!

In mid-August the Cubby Hole went into decline. It would still produce when favoured by a warm south-easterly wind (the swim lay in the north-west corner of the lake), but was otherwise erratic. That was when I switched to my late summer swim – coincidentally almost diametrically opposite the Cubby Hole. I called it the In-Willows. Actually it wasn't a swim as such, merely a small gap in a line of willows which enabled access to a five-feet-wide strip of semi-clear sand-gravel margin, six to nine feet deep, which lay between the bank-side reeds and the dense weeds that grew down the margin slope. This relatively shallow water was in marked contrast to the Cubby Hole, incidentally, which comprised a fifteen- to seventeen-foot gentle slope at the base of an underwater hump.

The Cubby Hole and the In-Willows produced tench even when affected by the wrong wind – in other words, a wind that blew away from them. But if the wind blew in the wrong direction for more than two or three days, both became unproductive, as tench drifted off to areas that received the positive effects of the wind. This is not to suggest that tench allow themselves to be shunted about a pit by every vagary of the wind, but they do respond to a warm wind that blows steadily for a sustained period. The key time, I have found, is day three and beyond. On the first day of a new wind, one or two tench may drift into an

affected area. The second day, a few more drift in. The third day, I would expect fish to arrive in numbers – and they will stay for as long as conditions prevail. When conditions change, they move back to their original holding areas. Interestingly, their 'return home' response is virtually instantaneous, quite unlike the leisurely pace of their initial movement on the wind.

Will groundbait hold them? Not in my opinion. Indeed, I think the effects of groundbaiting (and prebaiting, for that matter) are vastly overrated – it may make a good spot better, but I've never known it draw fish into an area they wouldn't otherwise have chosen, nor will it hold them once they decide to move. I'm talking here of moderate amounts of feed (up to about two kilos per day). I've no experience of massive quantities comprising gallons of maggots and casters and bucketfuls of hemp, so I am unable to comment on its effectiveness, although I've heard accounts of some prodigious catches taken by such means.

Before moving on, there is one final comment I want to make about tench location. Angling literature is full of references to tench as a 'mud-loving fish'. I disagree, and I think Dick Walker best summed it up when he wrote: 'The fact that tench will tolerate mud doesn't necessarily mean that they like it.' Mind you, their tolerance can be quite remarkable; take the description of Munden Hall in Essex by William Yarrell in *A History of British Fishes* (1836): '…the mud was intolerably faetid, and had dyed the fish of its own colour, which was that of ink…'.

Notwithstanding the fact that tench will tolerate mud, and will feed on and even in it, I've little doubt that, given the choice, they prefer sand or gravel. Second- and third-generation gravel pits rarely have significant silt deposits, but first-generation pits usually do. And in my experience, you'll catch many more tench from hard-bottomed swims than from areas where silt has accumulated.

THE INFLUENCE OF THE WEATHER

My wife considers I'm obsessed by weather forecasts. Until recently it involved channel hopping on the television, coupled with recourse to Teletext and Ceefax; nowadays it's weather websites on the Internet that get my attention.

Weather forecasts are important. Not only do they influence which water I will fish, but also my choice of swim. Suppose, for example, I plan to arrive at about 7am. There is a very good chance that little wind will have established itself by that time, but if I know that, say, a brisk south-easterly will pick up in the late morning, I'll have a very good idea of which water to choose and what swim I shall want to be in. On the

other hand, the forecast might promise variable winds, in which case I'll select a holding swim. A broiler of a day with a sunny flat calm requires either a holding swim, or a spot that fishes well in the margins. Then again, it might forecast cloudy, cool weather accompanied by a big north-westerly; in which case I will probably switch my attention from tench to carp.

If the forecast promises thunderstorms – in fact it only has to suggest that they might occur – I won't go fishing at all. This has nothing to do with whether tench will feed or not, but simply because I'm scared of being welded to my chair by five hundred zillion volts of superheated electrical discharge! There isn't a fish big enough to persuade me to sit out of doors in a thunderstorm. And as for holding a 12ft carbon-fibre lightning conductor while the sky is being ripped asunder by nature at its most explosive – no chance! Only the dim or deluded would willingly do anything so daft! I'm not a hide-under-the-table sort –

One that took a bait in the margins in hot, sunny, flat calm conditions.

indeed I enjoy watching a storm from the relative safety of my house, or, even better, from inside my car (the Faraday Cage principle, and all that) – but I won't venture outside.

As to what constitutes ideal weather for tench fishing, I suspect it depends on the sort of water being fished. Although I've caught a few tench from estate lakes and clay pits, my experience of them is very limited – certainly much too limited to know if my preferences as regards tench weather apply to such waters. I suspect how we fish is relevant, too, in that a session angler might have different preferences to someone like myself who only fishes in the daytime. But as a daytime-only, gravel-pit angler, my top three preferences are as follows:

1. Sunny and warm; light to moderate wind from the south-east, south or south-west.
2. Intermittent cloud; warm wind as outlined in (1).
3. Cloud; warm wind as outlined in (1).

The common denominator in my list is the word 'warm'. I'm not suggesting that tench won't feed in cool conditions, but they feed with much greater enthusiasm when the air temperature is above 20°C; above 22° is better still.

Many anglers claim to have noticed a correlation between atmospheric pressure and the way fish feed, but frankly, I can't see it. A fish only has to swim a few inches higher or lower in the water to experience greater pressure variations than it would encounter through the whole range indicated by a barometer. Besides, it is impossible to divorce atmospheric pressure from the weather that accompanies it.

Although moon phases don't fall within the category of 'weather', I nonetheless think this might be a suitable juncture to comment on how they might affect tench activity and feeding. Frankly, I've never given much credence to the idea that moon phases had any discernible effect. Imagine my surprise, then, when I came across a scientific study that indicated a correlation between tench activity and bright moonlight. Seemingly, night activity was most pronounced during periods of full moon. Daytime activity also differed depending on the moon phase, but such differences were not significant.

It would seem, then, that the moon does have an effect, but insufficient to have a great deal of relevance to our fishing.

TIMING

When I wrote my book *Tench* (Beekay Publishers, 1990) I listed tench feeding times in order of preference as follows:

1. Morning, 7.00am to 12.00 noon.
2. Early afternoon, 12.00 noon to 3.30pm.
3. Early morning, dawn to 7.00am.
4. Late afternoon, 3.30pm to 6.00pm.
5. Evening, 6.00pm to dusk.
6. Night.

Now, fourteen years and very many tench later, I think the list still holds good, except that I would swap numbers three and four around, and put late afternoon ahead of early morning.

The reader might be surprised at the low ranking I give to early morning and late evening – after all, they are traditional tench times, are they not? Traditional times they may be, but they don't apply to gravel pits. I recall trying to expand the fishing time available to me by fitting in two or three pre-work trips per week. I got up ludicrously early in the morning, about 4am, packed an electric shaver, a toothbrush and a change of clothes, and belted down to one of several local pits. I was generally in my pitch and fishing by about 5am. Yes, I caught a few tench by following this debilitating routine, but time and again it would get to about 7.30am – the latest I dared stay if I was to get to work on time – when I would see the first tench rolling over my groundbait! It says a lot for my conscientiousness that, despite the temptation to canvas my system for an ailment that would justify my phoning in and taking a 'sickie', I never succumbed!

With early mornings generally proving unproductive, and leaving me completely exhausted into the bargain, I decided to switch to after-work trips. On a good day, with no after-school activities to supervise, I could get to the water by about 5.30pm, whereupon I would fish through until dusk. Evening trips were less debilitating than early mornings, but they were no more productive – indeed, they were marginally less so, if anything.

So, like almost everyone else, I had to rely on weekends and holidays. In this regard, though, I was fortunate in that my long summer holiday – late July through to the beginning of September – fell at a good time for tench fishing. Not perfect, mind – mid-July through to the end of September would have been better! Nowadays I only work part-time, so I can get to the water as often as I wish.

Night fishing, you will have noticed, falls at the very bottom of my list. You may be thinking that as a self-declared daytime-only angler, I'm not in a position to judge – which would be true, were it not for the fact that such was not always the case. Back in the days when I was a proper specimen hunter (which I define as looking ever so serious and earnest in trophy pictures, and when phrases such as 'rod hours' slipped effortlessly from my tongue!) I fished at night. And more often

than not, my baits lay untouched until after 7am. So why did I keep doing it? Because it's what specimen hunters did, that's why!

BAIT

Small Worms

My favourite tench bait is without doubt a **gilt-tail worm**. They are similar in size and appearance to redworms, with the difference that the last centimetre or so of the tail is bright yellow. I'm not talking 'yellow-ish' – you sometimes see that on ordinary redworms – but really vivid yellow.

Now for the bad news: you cannot buy them, nor can you breed them. The only way of obtaining gilt-tails is to cultivate the acquaintance of a pig farmer, and ask to dig in his muckheap. Don't dig too far from the edge of the heap or you will get brandlings, which, despite their frequent recommendation in angling literature, are a very poor bait. Dig near the periphery, where the temperature is somewhat lower, and you will unearth loads of redworms – and among the redworms, just occasionally, you will come across a gilt-tail.

Redworms are an excellent bait, second only to gilt-tails. They are more readily available, too, making it unnecessary to forage in pigs' muck! Many tackle shops sell them; they can also be obtained by mail order. Until recently, I bred my own. In my garden I had a large compost bin in which I put kitchen vegetable waste such as potato peelings, carrot tops, onion skins and cabbage stalks, and occasionally I put grass cuttings in there, too – though not often, or they caused the compost to overheat and become colonized by brandlings. Now and again I tore up a corrugated cardboard box and put that in, so the worms could burrow in the tunnels caused by the corrugations. When my sons were young we kept guinea pigs and rabbits, and the soiled straw from hutch clear-outs also went in.

My references to my redworm stock, you will notice, are in the past tense – and thereby hangs a sad tale! The summer before last my wife complained that my compost bin was the source of innumerable tiny fruit flies, like little thunder bugs. They didn't bite, or do anything similarly antisocial, but it was disconcerting to have them settle on washing when it was hung out to dry. Occasionally they came in the house, too. To make matters worse, my wife suspected that our next-door neighbours were being similarly afflicted. Reluctantly, I agreed that the compost bin would have to go. It broke my heart to dispose of a worm stock that was so well established that it formed a mass which closely resembled spaghetti bolognaise; but domestic harmony had to take precedence. So now I have to buy my worms.

Redworms will colonize a compost bin naturally, but the process will get underway more quickly if a starter stock is introduced. On no account should compost accelerators be used, as they will inhibit colonization. The only maintenance necessary is to keep the compost well watered, because if it dries out the worms will die.

From my disparaging references to **brandlings**, it is obvious that I don't rate them at all. They can be identified by means of very obvious mustard-yellow bands encircling their body. Redworms have these, too, but they are much more discreet. Occasionally you encounter worms that have wider bands than are found on redworms, but narrower than those on brandlings. Such worms look like hybrids, and I suspect they might be, because hybridization is not unknown among annelids. Hybrids or not, I call them '**redlings**'. I've caught tench on

them, but prefer not to use them if I have proper redworms available.

Dendrobaenas look like big redworms (although tougher and livelier) and are rated highly by many anglers, including my son. I've only used them occasionally as I've hitherto had plenty of redworms available, but my recently changed circumstances (I feel sad at the thought) and my reliance on mail-order worms will doubtless change all that. Dendrobaenas are tremendously hardy, and will last for weeks if kept somewhere cool.

Gilt-tails, redworms and dendrobaenas are hooked head-end only.

Lobworms

The down side of gilt-tails and redworms is that they are somewhat fragile, so are unsuitable for long casting. They are relatively small baits, too, so require the use of a small hook (size 12 being my usual choice). Dendrobaenas withstand casting somewhat better, and being larger, can be used on a size 10. But when I want to cast a long way, or need the strength of a size 8 hook, I prefer a 5–6cm length of the head section of a lobworm. Old angling books always specify the tail of a lob, but I find the head end tougher and better able to withstand hard casting. I pass the hook through the non-severed end of the head, and out of the side.

Cockles and Clams

For many years, these were my secret bait! I have caught lots of big tench on cockles. Two on a hair combined with a size 8 hook is about right. You need fresh cooked or frozen cockles, incidentally, not those that are sold in vinegar.

Clams – or to be more precise, deep-water clams – are often sold as cockles. They are, however, a separate species, but

No doubt about what this one took! My 'secret' bait can be clearly seen.

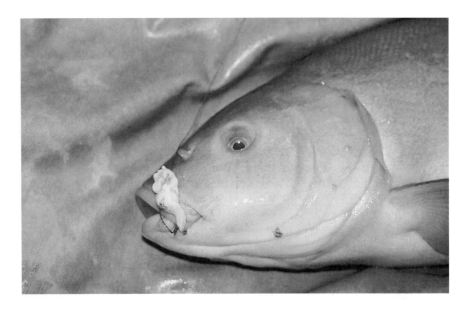

other than being slightly smaller are virtually identical. I presume they live below the low tide mark – hence the name – and are harvested due to many traditional cockle beds being fished out.

Cockles and clams can be bought from fishmongers and from some supermarkets, but I buy them by the gallon bucket from Whitstable fish market. They freeze well, so when I get them home I bag them up in single trip quantities (a large coffee mugful) and store them in my bait freezer.

The only problem with cockles and clams is that they go off very quickly in warm weather, so need to be taken to the waterside frozen in a wide-necked vacuum flask.

Prawns

Another one of my 'seafood specials'! I use the peeled variety, which I buy ready frozen from my local supermarket; again, I bag them up in single trip amounts and store them in my freezer. Their down side is that they are very fragile, so they need to be cocooned in PVA tape in order to

withstand casting. One on a hair is sufficient, with the tail of the prawn adjacent to a size 8 hook.

Like cockles, they go off quickly in warm weather, so need to be kept chilled.

They are expensive, but tench love them.

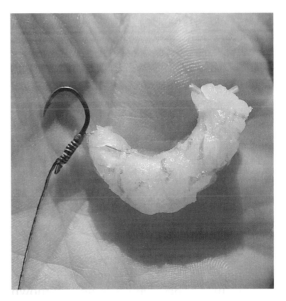

Prawns are fragile and expensive, but tench love them.

Boilies

Received wisdom has it that tench have a sweet tooth (if we are going to be pedantic about it, I suppose we should say 'sweet pharyngeal'!). For this reason, the usual boilies recommended for tench are those flavoured with strawberry, or peach or suchlike. However, this argument is flawed on two counts. First, synthetic flavours are not sweet – most, in fact, taste very bitter. And second, although tench do like sweet baits, they like savoury versions, too.

One of my all-time favourite tench boilies was a carp-style fishmeal recipe that contained a natural seafood extract. I use the past tense because the company from whom I bought the extract has ceased trading and I have been unable to locate the product elsewhere. It isn't a desperate loss, though, because there are very few carp boilies, that aren't taken with enthusiasm by tench. That said, I have my favourites. If I had to pick just one, I think it would be Nashbait Scopex Squid. But as I said, most boilies are effective, just so long as they don't contain garlic. Tench will take garlic-flavoured boilies, but not with any great enthusiasm.

Although I've occasionally caught tench on 20mm boilies, I prefer 15mm or smaller. One 15mm boilie or two 10–12mm boilies on a hair, combined with a size 8 hook is my choice.

Ninety per cent of the time I fish with standard bottom baits. I'm not a great fan of pop-ups and tend to restrict their use to those occasions when I need to overcome a layer of bottom silkweed, or, less frequently, when compelled to fish over soft silt. My brother Rick, on the other hand, rates mini pop-ups very highly indeed, and has caught some very big tench on them (including a couple of double-figure fish).

When fishing Method style, I often use hookbaits made from my Method mix. The hookbaits are then perfectly compatible with the groundbait. No flavours are added, just two tablespoons of liquid molasses per six eggs. The dry Method-mix groundbait is first given a quick spin in a blender to break down any large lumps, then mixed to a paste with beaten eggs. Finally it is rolled out into 10mm-thick

Preparation of boilie cubes. Extra molasses has made the baits very dark.

slices, boiled for 1½ minutes, then cut into cubes. I use two cubes on a hair in conjunction with a size 8 hook.

Pellets

Like most cyprinids, tench love trout, salmon and halibut pellets, and I use them for both hookbait and feed. The best were salmon pellets (past tense because they have become difficult to obtain) that could be drilled out so they could be mounted on a hair. Trout and halibut pellets can be drilled out, too, but they disintegrate in the water too quickly to make them a viable hookbait. They last a bit longer if secured by an elasticized pellet band, but I'm not keen on the system because to my eyes it looks somewhat obtrusive. I'm extremely fussy about how my rigs and presentations look – they have to be discreet, and must fulfil rigorous criteria for neatness. I'm being serious here; my rigs have to look right.

An alternative to drilling is to Superglue two pellets back-to-back with the hair sandwiched between them. I've never tried it, but my son has, and he reckons it works well.

Fortunately there is a solution – leastways, there is for me, though I regret to say that it won't be of much help to you! Brian Smith, a friend of mine, managed to obtain a supply of the now discontinued Van den Eynde semi-hard hookbait pellets (trout pellet flavour), which he generously shared with me. It is unfortunate that they are no longer made because they are excellent; Brian and I have caught a lot of tench on them.

Particles

The most widely used particle bait is sweetcorn. Its only disadvantage is that it is too fragile to withstand a heavy impact with the water surface, such as when casting a Method ball. This problem is easily overcome by using sweetcorn in the groundbait, but cooked maize on the hook: two grains of maize on a hair in conjunction with a size 8 hook is a good combination. Many carp anglers use artificial corn, but I can't get my head round the notion of fishing with plastic baits. Besides, I've no confidence that tench would prove to be as undiscerning as carp in this regard!

I've caught a lot of tench on black-eyed beans, cooked as per Rod Hutchinson's original recipe in double-strength tomato soup. I've also caught them on maple peas and chickpeas.

It goes without saying that all particle baits should be properly cooked before use to ensure they don't swell up inside the fish's gut and cause problems.

I use two on a hair in conjunction with a size 8 hook.

Bread

Bread is an under-used bait – something I'm as guilty of as anyone else – which is surprising because tench like it. I mean, *really* like it. Another thing that commends its use is the fact that in the form of pinched flake or compressed crumb (like an over-size punch-pellet) it sinks very slowly and will settle with gossamer lightness on the softest weed or silt. It's versatile, too; for instance, a piece of crust can be anchored so that it presents off-bottom like a pop-up.

I have promised myself that I'll use it much more in future, especially for margin fishing, and I'm confident that I'll do well with it.

Maggots

You will notice that I've made no mention of maggots, which is surprising in view of the fact that they are probably the most popular tench bait in current use. I've caught tench on maggots, but in truth not very many. My minimal success is no reflection on their effectiveness, but simply the consequence of my having used them so seldom.

Paradoxically, despite my hardly ever using them as hookbait, they are a standard ingredient in my feed when feeder fishing.

Groundbait

I'll refer once again, if I may, to my Beekay *Tench* book. In it you'll find the following groundbait recipe (all measures by volume):

- Six measures of white crumb
- Two measures of layers' mash
- One measure of roast barley that has been kibbled (ground up but left in bits, not reduced to powder)
- One measure of fishmeal

Before continuing, I ought to explain that layers' mash is a ready-mixed chicken food, which is obtainable from animal feed suppliers and shops that specialize in selling pet food.

I used that mix not just for groundbait in the conventional sense, but also as a plug when using maggots and other loose feed in an open-ended swim-feeder. It served me extremely well and produced a lot of tench, but has now been superseded by Vitalin (a proprietary brand of dry dogfood). Vitalin forms a perfect consistency when mixed with lake water, and it is ideal for conventional groundbaiting, feeder plugging and Method fishing. For a few years it was on the 'secret list' and only used by those tench, carp and bream anglers who were 'in the know'. Now, however, everyone uses it.

I mix it up in relatively small batches

through the day, and take pains to keep it out of the sun – this, of course, to ensure freshness. Vitalin contains meat products, which once moistened will go off if allowed to get too warm.

Although it works well on its own, it is even better if various bits and pieces are added to it: pellets, cooked particles, maggots, hookbait samples and so on.

WEED PROBLEMS

In the early part of my contribution I described how eutrophication has massively increased the amount of weed in most gravel pits. First-generation pits, with few areas deeper than about ten feet, can be weeded from end to end; second-generation pits are likely to have extensive weed other than in areas deeper than about thirteen feet (although this varies, depending on the clarity of the water). Third-generation pits will probably be more or less clear of weed other than in sedimentary shallows or on the margin slope.

The main sorts of weed are milfoil and *Elodea*. Milfoil isn't too bad, but *Elodea* is awful stuff and tends to grow so thick that an inadvertent cast into a dense bed of it with 12lb line can result in a borderline pull-for-a-break situation. Weed affects both presentation and playing fish. We'll look at the second of those issues first.

Playing tench is problematic in weed. In my opinion, a 7lb weeded tench is more difficult to deal with than is a carp of two or three times the size. This is because carp, when they get weeded, will eventually try to fight their own way free, with the result that their struggles tear up the weed that envelops them. Tench, however, lie still. I think it's a situation not unlike that of a tame hawk or falcon with its head covered with a hood – it can't see, so it remains quiet. A weeded tench, with its eyes covered by weed, does the same. Landing a weeded tench, therefore, requires either that the fish be pulled from the weed, or more likely that the mass of weed which envelops it is ripped free of the surrounding bed. I'm not a fan of heave-and-haul fishing, but with weeded tench there is no choice. All too often I've had a run, struck, felt a preliminary tug or two, and have then been weeded solid. I've pulled until something has given, where-upon a great mass of weed has been drawn to the bank with little or no indication that there has been a fish wrapped inside. 'Playing' such fish is about as much fun as hauling in a weed rake. But there you have it; it's a fact of life when fishing heavily weeded pits.

The nature of the fishing makes light tackle a non-starter. Indeed, I go further and say that anyone who fishes with tackle of inadequate strength in this sort of situation is being wholly irresponsible because the line will inevitably snap and leave the poor tench trailing line and with a hook in its mouth.

This is a situation where carp tackle is required. I use 2.25lb test-curve rods (12ft Eclipses) in conjunction with either 12lb or 15lb line. There are those who will protest that such an outfit has no place in tench fishing. Ignore them. In thick weed, heavy tackle is essential.

Bait Presentation

In order to achieve good bait presentation we need to find clear spots, or at the very least, places where the weed is sparse enough to be fishable. It's a fortunate fact that even the weediest pits have clear spots. How many and how big varies from one water to another, but I've yet to encounter a pit where I couldn't find clear spots pro-viding I looked hard enough. How to find them? The only reliable way is by means of

Carp tackle was necessary to extract this one from thick weed.

a lot of diligent work with a plumbing rod. When I identify such places, I record details of distance and direction in a note-book.

I try to find four or five suitable swims in completely different areas of the pit, thereby enabling me to choose a swim in relation to the wind direction. And because there are several swims in my repertoire, it is highly improbable that I will arrive at the water and find them all occupied by other anglers. Weed encroachment on my clear spots is discouraged by baiting each of them two or three times per week – or whenever possible, depending on the pres-ence of other anglers – with about 250g of cooked hempseed and 100g or so of trout pellets. The consequent foraging by tench – and carp and bream if present – will help to keep the spots free of weed.

In view of the aforementioned difficulties involved in landing big tench from heavily weeded swims, I confine myself to fishing at relatively short range, up to a maximum of thirty-five yards or so. This is because, as already explained, tench are difficult to pull through thick weed, and if the fishing is done at too great a distance, the task of landing a fish will not be 'difficult', it will be impossible. On some waters, boats are used to free weeded fish, but on the pits that I fish, boats are not permitted. I therefore want to keep the amount of weed between the fish and me to a manageable level.

An added advantage of close-range fishing is that even modest-sized clear spots are viable targets.

Standard Weed Rig

My rigs are simple. I never add sliding or revolving components to my hook because they are unstable, and as a consequence unpredictable with regard to how the bait is presented and how the rig behaves when it is picked up by a tench. This is always assuming, of course, that it is picked up at all, because some 'advanced' rigs are so ungainly that I'm not surprised to read such comments as: 'The only baits left in my swim were the hookbaits – all the freebies had gone.' Carp anglers get away with ungainly rigs because carp, let it be whispered, are somewhat tolerant in this regard!

I use a relatively heavy wire, size 8 hook for most of my weedy-water tench fishing. My favourite pattern is the Owner spade-end. Some anglers, however, can't get along with spade-end hooks, in which case I suggest Gardner Talon Tip, Kamasan B982 or, if barbless patterns are preferred,

Mustad Eyed Stillwater Extra Power or Ashima C-415.

My beloved gilt-tails and redworms are unsuitable for this sort of fishing because they are incompatible with heavy wire hooks. Dendrobaenas are okay, with the last few millimetres of the tail nipped off to prevent them burying in the bottom. The head of a lob is good, too. Such baits are only of use, however, if the clear spot is truly clear; if there is any weed at all in the vicinity there is a risk of the worm tying itself up in it. Most of the time, therefore, I use boilies, cockles, prawns or particles, threaded on a fine, flexible hair made from Drima polyester sewing thread. The hair's pivot is located on the outside of the shank, directly opposite the hook point. To heighten the likelihood of my hookbait behaving like freebies, albeit to a limited degree, and to ensure that the bait doesn't mask the hook, I have 5mm clearance between the hook bend and the top of the bait.

A spade-end hook, which has the hook-link emerging from the front of the shank, contributes to efficient hook rotation, which in turn results in lower-lip hook-holds. The same effect is achieved with eyed hooks by means of the knotless knot or line aligner. This is important, because in addition to being more secure, lower lip hook-holds result in less mouth damage.

The hook-link comprises a combi-link made from 15lb Kryston Mantis. My combi-links are 35cm in length and have a 4–5cm section of exposed braid core adjacent to the hook. This is how they are made:

- Cut a 48cm length of Mantis.
- Soften 10cm of the coating by immersing it in a vacuum flask of very hot water.
- Withdraw the Mantis from the flask, and strip the softened coating with fingernails or child's plastic play scissors.

- Attach the hook to the stripped portion of core. The hair is secured by trapping it beneath the knot coils. Alternatively it may be attached afterwards by means of a needle knot.
- If required, a line aligner is added.
- A 3cm length of 1mm olive-green silicon tube is slid on to the hook-link.
- A size 12 swivel is attached.
- A tiny dab of superglue is touched to both hook-knot and swivel knot. Finally, when the glue is dry, the silicon tube is pushed over the swivel knot's tag end and the lower eye of the swivel.
- Mantis is neutral density, which is to say that it sinks, but only just. To ensure my hook-links lie flat on the bottom, I apply a couple of tiny 'mouse droppings' of Kryston Drop-Em.

For fishing in, or immediately adjacent to, weed I like an elongated 1.25oz in-line lead, because the combination of low mass and elongated shape successfully avoids hang-ups. It is used in conjunction with a 45cm length of lightly back-weighted No Spook anti-tangle tube.

In more benign situations where the weed is less severe, I might use a 1.25oz pendulum lead on a lead clip. There's no real reason for the different set-up, however, just pure whim!

I don't know how my rigs compare with those of my co-authors because I haven't seen their contributions, but I suspect their hook-links might be shorter. Certainly in *Tenchfisher* magazine (www.tenchfishers. net), many rig references describe hook-links of 10cm or less. Part of the current popularity of short hook-links might be due to the widespread use of maggots as hookbait (which, you may recall, I rarely use). I really don't know. All I'll say on the subject is that I find long hook-links effective. I'm not trying to convert anyone to my point of view; all I'm doing is explaining how I catch tench. If anyone reading this decides to go his or her own way and do something different, that's fine by me!

My standard weed rig: notice how the end of the PVA stringer cocoons the hook to reduce the risk of hang-ups as it sinks through weed.

Clipping Up

Unless my target area is very close – in which case I will simply lower or swing out the tackle – I will most likely resort to clipping up. The conventional way of doing this is to secure the line beneath the reel's line clip; however, I do not like this method for fear it will cause line damage. Some anglers minimize the risk by placing a Power-Gum or mono spacer beneath the clip, which serves the dual purpose of creating a buffer and reducing the pinching effect of the clip. My preference is for a system that does not require that the line be placed beneath the clip at all: instead, it is held in a Power-Gum harness, which is created by placing a Power-Gum loop on the spool before it is filled with line. The loop is just long enough to enable it to be tucked beneath the line clip. To utilize the loop for clipping up, it is detached from the line clip, the line is placed beneath it, and then it is re-attached. (If the foregoing brief description is not clear, you might find it helpful to read fuller details, with explanatory diagrams, in my book *Gravel Pit Carp* (Laneman, 1999).) While it may sound complicated, my method of clipping up is actually very straightforward in practice.

There is a knack to casting when clipped up. To prevent the line pulling tight in mid-air, which can result in the end-tackle rebounding and falling short, it is necessary to hold the rod high, almost vertical, and allow it to be pulled down to the horizontal by the momentum of the cast. The consequent shock-absorber effect should, providing the cast is not too hard (muscle memory comes into the procedure, too), result in the baited end-tackle falling just right.

Whatever system of clipping up is employed, it is essential to remember that the line must be removed from the clip before the rod is placed in the rests. Failure to do this is likely to result in, at best, a missed take, and at worst, a lost rod.

Range can be established, incidentally, by use of a brightly coloured pole-elastic line marker (as mentioned earlier when I described how I undertake swim-mapping).

Feeding the Swim

My usual procedure is to lob three tangerine-size groundbait balls per rod in the immediate vicinity of where I intend casting.

With groundbait in place, I then cast the end-tackles. Bite indication is provided by lightweight, long-arm swing-type indicators, which I allow to hang vertical. These are used in conjunction with Delkim alarms. The reels, Shimano Baitrunners, are set in free-spool mode. Everything is set up carp style, in fact.

I sit as close to my rods as circumstances allow, because I want to be able to strike as soon as a run gets under way. I aim to make contact before the tench has travelled much more than a yard, because the sooner I get a fish under control, the less opportunity it has to bury itself in weed.

Most takes are fliers. The alarm sounds and the indicator flies up to the horizontal. Occasionally it stays there and nothing else happens, but I strike nonetheless: this is because tench sometimes run straight to weed where they'll lie without moving. Most times, though, the run takes the conventional form whereby the reel spool spins and the Delkim warbles its little heart out!

METHOD TACTICS

The primary advantage of Method fishing is that it concentrates free feed in very close proximity to the hookbait, thereby –

if I may be forgiven for employing a jargon-style phrase – amplifying the food signal. Another benefit is that it is virtually 100 per cent tangle free. It also lends itself to fishing on, or in, certain types of weed.

These are the pluses. Unfortunately it has disadvantages too, the main one being that a heavy Method ball requires the use of a fairly stiff rod (a lemon-size ball, used in conjunction with a 1–2oz lead, weighs approximately 6–7oz). My 2.25lb test-curve Eclipses can cope with Method ball distances up to about thirty-five yards – providing the end-tackle is lobbed with a gentle overhead sweep rather than a conventional cast – but for greater distances I either have to reduce the size of the Method ball or resort to 2.75lb test-curve rods. As you will doubtless understand, I am reluctant to use such heavy rods for tench fishing, and only do so when I feel there's no other option.

Paradoxically, it's not just medium to long casting that creates difficulty; close-in fishing is awkward, too – unless it is so close that it can be lowered straight down. The weight of a lemon-size Method ball renders normal underarm casting impossible (sounds improbable, but try it and you'll see that I'm right). Again, a reduced size Method ball helps, as does a modified underarm casting style that involves holding the Method ball in the free hand (the non-rod hand) on a tight line, and swinging it out. Timing the precise moment of release is tricky, but it comes with practice. It is only possible to cast a couple of rod-lengths by this means, but often that's sufficient.

Another problem that soon becomes apparent when casting a Method ball is that it has an adverse effect on accuracy. In open water situations this may not matter too much, but when precision casting is required, such as when targeting clear spots in weed, or trying to drop in a

2.25lb test-curve rods are okay for Method fishing if the cast is slow and relatively gentle.

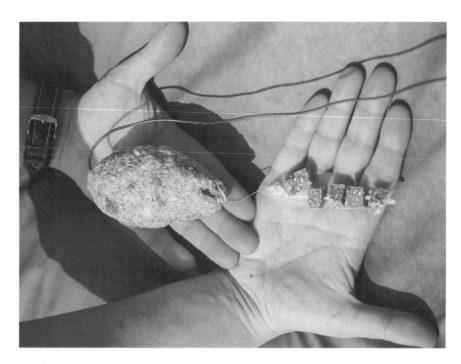

The business end of my Method set-up (note the groundbait-based boilie cubes for hookbait and stringer).

particular depth on the side of an island slope, a deviation of a yard or two might matter a great deal.

Method Rig

The rig I use for most of my Method fishing comprises a 1.25oz in-line lead used in conjunction with 45cm of lightly back-weighted No Spook anti-tangle tube. In association with semi-slack line, the back-weight holds the anti-tangle tube flat to the bottom, thereby rendering it less noticeable. It also reduces the incidence of line bites.

For longer casting distances, I swap the in-line lead for a Middy birdcage-type Method feeder, although I modify it by removing three of the feeder's six wires. Brother Rick found that this modification gave a more secure grip on the Method ball, and made it less likely to 'ski' along the bottom in response to subsurface drag on the line.

My Method hook-links are made from HPPE braid, 15lb Kryston Super-Nova being my favourite. As with my combi-links described earlier, I prefer them longer than normal; thus my Method hook-links are never shorter than 35cm, and are sometimes as long as 45cm. This is in stark contrast to most anglers who favour 10–15cm versions for Method fishing. I tried short hook-links but experienced a few aborted takes and hook pulls, so I reverted to my preferred long links.

Encasing the Link

A ball of groundbait is moulded to the required size and shape, then slit length-ways with the blunt edge of a knife blade, which enables it to be opened up like pitta bread. Inside this slit is placed the lead or Method feeder, followed by the hook-link, which is folded in an approximate 'Z' configuration with 3–5cm hanging clear. Finally the groundbait ball is closed and remoulded to its original lemon shape.

You might expect a hook-link that is folded back-and-forth to tangle, but it does not. When the groundbait ball disintegrates and a fish takes the bait, the hook-link straightens smoothly and without hang-up.

To ensure that my baited hook cannot foul the main line in flight, and to render a hair tangle impossible, I encase the hook and hair in a pellet of soluble foam (which you can buy either from a tackle shop, or by the sackful and at a fraction of the tackle-shop price, direct from packaging suppliers where it's called 'bio-degradable packaging foam'). Alternatively, if I'm using boilies, I might attach a stringer; as well as providing a few extra feed items adjacent to the hook-bait, it enhances the rig's tangle-free qualities.

Setting Up

After casting, the line is submerged and gently tightened. This should be done very carefully because a Method ball, although heavy in air, has a low specific gravity so is easily dislodged in water. This may cause it to disintegrate and allow the lead to be dragged along the bottom, resulting in the hookbait being pulled away from the feed – which defeats the purpose of the tactic. It might also cause the hook point to become masked by debris, which can be a particular difficulty in the autumn if the bottom is cluttered with leaves and dying weed.

Runs and Twitches

Most of my takes, as with the previous approach, are conventional runs, but occasionally I get twitchy takes that lift the indicator a few centimetres at a time. I strike at anything I believe to be a proper take, but ignore those I suspect are line bites. How to tell the difference? If the indicator rises, then starts falling back, it is most likely just a line bite. If it lifts and holds, it is probably a take. Occasionally the difference is less clearly defined, and my response depends more on intuition than interpretation.

Method Summary

Despite the publicity accorded the Method tactic, it is less widely used than you might expect. I suspect the reason has more to do with follow-my-leader fashion than anything else – if someone fishes Method style and does well, others follow suit. Otherwise it tends to be neglected.

Method fishing is somewhat crude. It requires heavy rods and heavy line (I generally use 15lb breaking-strain). And when fishing calm, shallow water, I flinch at the monstrous 'spudoosh' created by the Method ball as it smashes down on the surface. But notwithstanding its lack of subtlety, it is an extremely effective way of catching tench; sometimes it is the most effective tactic of all.

MARGIN FISHING

Talk 'margins', and most anglers think in terms of reeds, lilies and overhanging trees. While such spots are always worth a try, I've caught many tench from seemingly featureless stretches of bank. What is more surprising is just how close they will come. I recall my son telling me that when he fished the Linear Complex in Oxford, he would drop his baits in a couple of feet of water less than a yard from the bank, with just the last few inches of rod poking over the edge; yet still he got line bites from fish passing between his baited end-tackles and his rod tips!

In some extremely weedy waters, the only weed-free area of any significance is a strip just a few feet wide and up to about three feet deep, close to the bank. I assume it is kept weed free by swans, geese and other waterbirds grazing there. When the sun warms this shallow water, tench patrol along it, especially if the bank has a south-facing aspect.

Another classic margin situation is found in deep third-generation pits where dense weed grows down the margin slope. The outer edge of the weed – where it gives way to a clear bottom – is a prime patrolling area, and precise casting to a couple of feet beyond the weed-line can be a successful tactic.

In my Beekay book *Tench* I wrote the following: 'When it's hot, you should fish close; when it's not, don't.' A bit glib, I agree, but when applied to shallow margins it is good advice. Deeper margins, such as those described in the previous paragraph, can fish well in cooler weather, however.

Hang Loose

When margin fishing, I like to fish with slack lines. Sometimes I take this to extremes and have loose loops hanging between the rod rings. Something that makes me smile is the reaction of other anglers when they see me fishing in this manner, which more often than not is, 'Aren't your lines slack? I'd have no confidence fishing like that.'

To which my standard response is, 'Don't do it then!' Problem solved!

The reason I fish this way is because observation has shown me that if a tench swims into a slack line, the line slowly draws taut, then, more often than not, slips free of the tench's body – and the fish shows no sign of being alarmed. Contrast that with what happens if it swims into a tight line; the last you'll see of it is a spook-swirl as it flees in panic.

Margin fishing, and I'm nicely tucked out of sight behind cover.

My usual rod-rest set-up: wide diameter banksticks and extra strong angle-steel buzzer-bars.

If I judge a slack line to be inappropriate – for instance, where the bottom is strewn with flints or mussels that might damage it – I fish instead with what I call a droopy line, whereby it hangs in a gentle arc.

Rod-Rest Assemblies

This seems as good a time as any to offer my thoughts on rod-rest assemblies. Some gravel pits have rock-hard banks that resist banksticks. There are three ways of dealing with this problem, the first of which involves the use of a mallet to hammer banksticks into the ground. What can I say? Anyone who expects tench to feed after such disturbance is at best a wide-eyed innocent, or at worst plain stupid.

A better option is a **rod-pod**. Its main disadvantage is that it requires a relatively benign swim to be practical. Very steep swims, or those which require that rods be set up in watery margins, aren't really pod-friendly. And compared with a bankstick set-up, a pod isn't particularly stable.

Which brings me to my preferred system: **interchangeable wide-diameter banksticks** in various lengths (2ft to 5ft). Their advantage, apart from their stability and strength, is that they afford sufficient friction to resist turning (other than in loose shingle).

If combined with a really strong buzzer bar – I like Chris Brown's angled steel version – the bar can be gripped in both hands and used to force the bankstick into the ground.

Where the ground is so hard that it resists any attempt to push banksticks in, I use a screw-threaded auger with which I drill suitable holes. Gardner Tackle produce an auger for this very purpose, or a screw-ended bankstick may be used (such as the Nash Powerstick or Dinsmore Power Drive).

I own a pod, but the only time I use it is when fishing from a platform – although even then, if the margins aren't too deep I prefer to use my longest banksticks and set up my rods alongside the platform.

Keep the faith ... even tench as big as this one will come into extremely shallow margins.

Keep the Faith

Few anglers have much confidence in margin fishing. This creates a self-perpetuating negative dynamic in that if no one believes it to be an effective approach, no one tries it. Because no one tries it, no tench are caught this way, which reinforces the belief that it is unproductive... and so on. It is easy to lose confidence and quit when faced with that sort of thing, but those who 'keep the faith' and persevere will eventually succeed. And it's worth persevering,

because margin fishing isn't merely an alternative, idiosyncratic approach for traditionalists and eccentrics, far from it; in the right circumstances it is an extremely effective way of catching tench.

It's exciting, too! Even though I have caught many tench from the margins, I still experience momentary panic when my rod tip stabs round to the accompaniment of a heart-racing 'Beeeeeep!' from my alarm. Wonderful stuff!

FEEDER FISHING

Thus far my tactics have been chosen with weedy pits in mind, but just occasionally we encounter one that is relatively weed free. It may be due to the pit being too young for weed to have become properly established, or where weed is inhibited by water that is too deep, turbid or coloured by algae to allow adequate light penetration. Or maybe the controlling club has got rid of the weed by treating the water with an aquatic weedkiller (this should only be done under the supervision of a qualified fishery management consultant). There's one other possibility, and it's something that doesn't happen often, but is by no means unknown. It occurs when weed proliferates to such an extent that it uses up all the available nutrients. This results in a weed-free year; sometimes a couple of consecutive weed-free years, until the nutrient supply recovers and the weed becomes re-established.

I encountered precisely this circumstance five or six years ago on Johnson's Island Lake. Normally the lake is heavily weeded, but throughout the year in question it was confined to well defined areas. The rest of the pit was more or less clear. But here's a strange thing. Those who know Johnson's will be aware that the Island and Road Lakes are connected by a quite substantial channel, substantial enough to fuel arguments as to whether they qualify as two lakes or should be regarded as just one. With the Island Lake having become all but free of weed, it would seem logical to expect the Road Lake to be likewise. But it wasn't. Other than in the deepest areas, it was choked with the stuff! I tried a bit of weed clearing in one of my erstwhile favourite Road Lake swims, but all I achieved after ninety minutes' hard work was to become sweat-soaked and mud-spattered! Oh yes, I extracted an impressive pile of weed, but made really no impression at all on the weed in the swim!

Anyway, back to the plot. When, for whatever reason, we find ourselves fishing a weed-free pit, we can use proper tench tackle! While I will readily use carp tackle and carp-style tactics to catch tench when I have to, I much prefer it when I can fish with, say, 1.25lb test-curve rods and 5lb breaking-strain line. Or if the water isn't completely weed free, but has patches here and there, I ratchet up to 1.75lb test-curve rods and 8lb breaking-strain line.

Feeder Rig

The most enjoyable, and in my experience the most productive form of light-line tench fishing, is with swim-feeders. When I started feeder fishing I experimented with a number of different arrangements, most of which incorporated swivels in their assembly. None was entirely satisfactory, the main problem being one of tangles. The answer came from an unlikely source – well, two unlikely sources, actually: Ivan Marks and Kevin Ashurst. The reason I describe them as being unlikely sources is because they were match anglers – indeed, back in the 1970s they were *the* match anglers, such was their domination.

Their chosen rig comprised a long hook-link, to which was knotted a short bomb-link. There were no swivels, beads, sliding rings or booms, and the basic set-up appealed to me because it was so simple (I subscribe to the KISS principle: Keep It Simple, Stupid!).

This is how it is assembled. Approximately 100cm from the end of the line and using a separate length of mono, a four-turn sliding stop knot or a sliding grinner knot is attached. It is tied so its uppermost tag end (that is, the one nearest the rod tip) is about 30cm in length; this will form the bomb/feeder-link. The lower tag end can be trimmed off so it is only a couple of millimetres long.

By using the upper tag end for the bomb-link, the knot coils lock in position and the link won't slip – not readily, anyway. If it does, re-tie it with more turns, five or even six, instead of the four I have suggested. The only down side of using more turns is that the knot won't tighten so easily, and extra care needs be taken to ensure the main line is not damaged.

My favourite feeder is the largest size Drennan Feederlink. I like the similarly designed Middy Feeder, too. I dispense with the integral nylon link and the detachable cap, and use the feeder upside down (that is, with its open end pointing downwards). The bomb-link is passed through the central hole in the closed end of the feeder, and passed out of the open end to enable a weight to be attached (the Middy version is self-weighted). Often I use nothing more than a swan shot or two, but if there is a troublesome cross-wind or significant subsurface flow, I'll use a bored bullet. The weight is then pulled back inside the feeder so it butts up against the closed end.

The set-up is neat, simple and tangle free. In addition – and I think this is important – by attaching the hook directly to the end of the main line, there is no intervening knot to compromise the line's breaking strain. Retaining maximum line strength is important when we are fishing light because there's little or no inherent safety margin.

Bait and Feed

My favourite light-line hook is Kamasan's B980 (which, for some inexplicable reason, is becoming less readily available than it used to be), size 12 or 10, depending what bait I'm using. My normal choice is a small worm, but if bootlace eels, small perch or skimmer bream prove to be a problem I switch to something like hair-rigged cooked maize or hook pellet.

The feeder is stuffed with maggots, cooked hempseed, a chopped worm or two, a few grains of sweetcorn and some mini pellets. The feeder's open end is then plugged with groundbait to retain it all in place.

Casting and Striking

To encourage the line to sink immediately it makes contact with the water, and thereby prevent it from bellying in a crosswind, I carry a small dropper bottle of dilute washing-up liquid, which is applied to the spool periodically through the day.

My indicator set-up is the same as previously described, the only difference being that I don't have the reels in free-spool. Nor do I engage the anti-backwind. If a very fast take occurs, the reel may spin briefly, but it's a simple matter to grab the rod and at the same time drop a finger on the flier to stop it.

The long hook-link (approximately 100cm) results in lovely sail-away bites, which is not only more relaxing than hovering over the rod trying to hit tiny millimetric twitches, I think it's more

efficient, too. The only problem sometimes experienced with the long hook-link is that bites can be too confident, with the result that fish are sometimes deep hooked. If that happens, it is merely necessary to shorten it down to 75cm, or even 50cm.

LINE FACTS

While discussing feeder fishing, I made reference to fine lines and the need to retain as much of the line's breaking-strain as possible, and I feel that the subject is sufficiently important to warrant a section in its own right.

The first thing to realize is that the actual breaking strain of a line might be higher or lower than that stated on the spool, likewise the diameter. This means that nominal test-strength and diameter should be taken only as a guide, and not used to compare one brand with another. For comparisons to be meaningful we need to undertake spring-balance and micrometer tests of our own.

We also need to be aware of the fact that, broadly speaking, there are three types of line: general 'workhorse' lines (which I shall refer to as 'GW'), those which have a low diameter in relation to breaking strain (which I shall call LD), and those which have an extremely low diameter in relation to their breaking strain (ULD – as in 'ultra low diameter').

GW lines are tough, durable and tolerant of most knots. You could tie a 'running half granny' in them and it would be okay (there's no such knot, I just made it up to illustrate how tolerant are lines in this category!). GW lines tend to be somewhat stretchy, too. My personal choice in this category is Berkley Big Game, since its characteristics make it ideal for heavy-duty work such as Method fishing.

Big tench fight hard, so 100 per cent reliable line is essential. (I'm not sure what caused the mark on this fish's flank – I suspect a cormorant stab.)

LD lines are ideal for most sorts of fishing. They are strong for their diameter, highly abrasion-resistant, have medium stretch, are supple, and have low memory. My favourites are Nash Bullet and Sufix Magic Touch.

ULD lines have relatively little stretch (in mono terms, that is), and they are extremely fussy about which knots they'll take. I use ULD lines for light-line feeder fishing, my favourite being Shimano Exage.

You will notice that I have made no mention of braid main line, and that is because I don't like it. It is prone to casting tangles, it has virtually no stretch so puts excessive strain on hook-holds, and to my eyes it looks too conspicuous. And besides, I'm happy with mono.

Knots

We are all familiar with knot illustrations on line packaging, but I have to tell you that such information often relies on assumptions rather than tested fact. One commonly held belief, for example, is that a twice-through-the-eye knot will be stronger than once-through-the-eye versions. Yes, sometimes it is, but often it isn't. Most ULD and some LD monos are actually stronger at the knot when the line is passed just once through the eye of the swivel or hook. Okay, I know it doesn't make sense, but it's so; if you doubt me, conduct your own tests.

Another commonly held view is that barrel-type knots (for example uni/grinner, clinch, half-blood and so on) require five or more turns for maximum strength. Again, it depends on the brand of mono; most ULD and some LD versions achieve maximum strength with just four turns. And here's another surprise: the frequently maligned half-blood is stronger in some ULD monos than are the uni/grinner and the clinch.

As an alternative to barrel-type knots there are those that rely on a bight (loop) being passed through the eye prior to being formed. The best known of this type is the palomar. Anyone who finds the intricacies of knot-tying difficult, and wants to rely on just one, should choose the palomar. It is easy to tie, and it works well in all types of mono. It is not necessarily the best knot, but it is consistently good.

Finally there is the knotless knot: only suitable for hooks, of course, and even then it can only be employed when the hook is being attached to a separate hook-link. Providing care is taken to ensure that the line passes across the blind (closed) side of the hook-eye, this is an excellent knot. Like the palomar, it works well in all types of mono.

Superglue

I always apply superglue to a knotless knot. This is because I very rarely utilize the hook-link tag end to create a hair (as mentioned earlier, I tie in a fine hair made from sewing thread), so without superglue there would be a risk of my knotless knot unravelling.

Superglue is applied to all my knots in HPPE braid (Super-Nova, Merlin, Super-Silk and so on) because this material is inherently slippery, which in turn increases the likelihood of the knot being weakened due to strangulation. Superglue prevents slippage and consequent constriction.

Having experimented with superglue on uni/grinner, clinch, half-blood and palomar knots in mono, I have concluded that there is no advantage to be gained. Nor does it do any harm – it does not, as has been suggested, make some monos go brittle. But if there is no benefit to be gained from applying superglue to an already good knot, I see little point in doing so.

Fluorocarbon

I can't leave the subject of lines without mentioning fluorocarbon. I've been disappointed in low diameter versions (up to, say, 0.25mm) in that their actual breaking strain tends to be as much as 20 per cent lower than that claimed on the spool. Furthermore, I've not found fluorocarbon to be particularly knot-friendly, and having lost confidence in it, I no longer use it.

The foregoing comments apply to 100 per cent fluorocarbon, not to fluorocarbon-coated copolymer lines such as P-Line and Krystonite. My bench tests on both of these have produced very good results, but I'll hold back a final opinion until I've used them for actual fishing.

WINTER TENCH

The traditional tench season is a relatively short one. Reports in the angling weeklies demonstrate this with unambiguous clarity. Tench captures peak in June, slow down a bit in July, slow down yet further in August and September, and are as rare as rocking horse manure (to paraphrase one of brother Rick's expressions!) in autumn.

Wouldn't it be nice if we could extend the tench season and catch them in winter? Well, we can, but when the viability of winter tench fishing is examined in detail, the picture that emerges is far from clear. I'll start the discussion by recounting my experiences in the winters of 1998/99, and 1999/2000. I had been lured to a local lake by stories of double-figure bream caught by carp anglers. As it transpired, the bream fishing was productive but disappointing. Method fishing with cockles or peeled prawns produced plenty of fish in the 6lb to 8lb category, and eighteen 9lb-pluses, but I topped out at 9lb 12oz. I concluded that the 'doubles' were probably eight- and nine-pounders that had benefited from enhanced weight estimation!

In addition to the bream (and inadvertent carp caught at the approximate rate of one per three trips) I caught six tench: four in my first winter, and two in my second. My son, Peter, had a couple, too. They came from the swim that produced all my carp and the bulk of my bream, the side of a gentle slope that fell from about nine feet down to approximately twenty feet. All eight tench came in January – and while the weather was fairly mild, it wasn't especially so.

I've had similar out-of-the-blue winter tench captures from other waters, the strangest of which occurred on Larkfield Two (this was back in the days when it was a Leisure Sport venue). They were proper winter fish – December and January – which was memorable enough, but what really made them stand out was the fact that on each trip they came at the same time, 3.00pm. Interestingly, too, it or they (I had one or two per trip) were generally preceded or followed by a carp. I'd sit there all day without a bleep from my alarms, only to have the first of two or three runs occur between 2.50pm and 3.10pm!

Some waters go further, and not content with occasional out-of-the-blue tench, produce them steadily all through the winter. One such was (and may still be, for all I know) Mote Park near Maidstone. This lake has a long and interesting history, including Alfred Jardine's erstwhile record 37lb pike (often wrongly attributed to Leeds Castle moat near Hollingbourne).

When I fished Mote Park for pike in the company of Len Burgess and Martin Gay, we didn't catch anything to rival Jardine's fish, but we enjoyed some excellent fishing and caught mid-doubles most trips.

In those far-off days (late 1970s or early 1980s, I would guess) I used live baits – a confession I make with some shame because, frankly, I think it is an indefensible practice. In order to supplement my bait supply, I fished with a maggot-baited float or feeder rod in addition to my pike rods. Len and Martin did likewise. And most trips, our roach-cum-skimmer rods produced one or two tench between us (these were not, I hasten to add, used as live bait!). From memory, they were caught independently of the weather in that they came in cold as well as mild conditions.

Brother Rick used to winter-fish a small Essex gravel pit that lay within sight of Thames saltwater creeks. He fished there for carp (with considerable success), but while so doing caught plenty of tench – two or three per day being the norm. After dark the catch rate increased yet further. Interestingly, following a freeze-up, the first fish to be caught when the ice cleared were tench!

Another of Rick's waters is a spring-fed, very shallow lake where tench remain active through the coldest midwinter conditions. Some days they group together and can be seen as a large dark mass lying on or near the bottom; other days they cruise and roll just like they would in high summer!

Two significant things have struck Rick regarding winter tench in this water: first, they feed better at night than in the daytime; and second, they keep to quite clearly defined areas of the lake.

Further to the night-fishing theme: back in the 1980s when Johnson's Lakes were in their heyday, one of the most successful anglers on the complex was a teacher from London. He was mad keen and fished every weekend all through the winter, even in the most atrocious conditions. He caught tench steadily, some big ones, too. Significantly, although he fished round the clock, almost all his fish came at night. Something else that might be significant is that he caught them on maggots.

Clearly a winter fish, but I reckon the jury is still out on whether winter tench fishing is worthwhile.

During the same period, erstwhile barbel record holder, Bob Morris, wrote an article about catching winter tench on maggots. In it he described how he and his father fished Leisure Sport's Sutton-at-Hone House Lake, and caught tench at night using, if I remember correctly, torch-on-float tactics.

I could quote other instances, but I think the foregoing will serve to indicate that winter tench fishing can be a viable proposition. Notice I said 'can be', not 'is', because I reckon the jury is still out as to whether winter tench – exceptional waters apart – are worth pursuing. It's immensely satisfying when it works, though.

56

OMISSIONS AND PHILOSOPHY

Nowhere in my contribution is there any reference to PVA bags. When I'm using dry loose feed such as pellets, powders and boilies, I put them in a PVA bag, which I attach to the hook. And I've caught plenty of tench by this means. Most of my feeding, however, comprises or incorporates wet items such as cockles, prawns, worms, sweetcorn and cooked particles, and I find it more convenient to include these in groundbait.

Nor is there any mention of the lift method, which some will see as an unforgivable omission because it is a technique which is synonymous with tench. The fact is, I've not found it to be a particularly effective way of catching them, but that probably has more to do with my inability to master the technique, rather than any inherent shortcomings it may have.

An even more glaring omission is that of float fishing in general. But again, it's not a technique I use to any great extent – leastways, not for tench.

Nor will you find accounts of session fishing, heavy groundbaiting, pre-baiting, or the use of massive swim-feeders. They are omitted because they are not in my repertoire.

Another omission concerns the weights of most of the fish in my photographs. That's not a result of my being coy or excessively modest, but quite simply because I'm unable to remember. Either that, or they weren't weighed in the first place.

Back in the days when I was a hardcore specimen hunter, every fish of note was weighed, and it was done with a great deal of solemnity, too! But nowadays, if the configuration of the bank permits it, the majority of my tench are unhooked in the landing net while still in the water, and released immediately.

My somewhat casual attitude to weighing them should not be taken to mean that

Most of my tench, like this one, are unhooked in the landing net, in the water, and are released immediately.

Big sky tench!

I am indifferent about the size of tench I catch. I may smile at the excesses and absurdities of the erstwhile specimen-hunting movement, but I'm still a specimen hunter at heart. But while my tench fishing is about big fish, it isn't necessarily about the biggest. I like mystery and I love pioneering. I would much rather fish a neglected water for unknown tench of unknown size, than add my name to the list of those who have caught a known double-figure specimen. Not that I'm very likely to catch a double-figure tench, known or unknown, because I feel somewhat uncomfortable about fishing for spawn-bloated females. I'm not claiming that I've never done it, but it's not something I've done very often. Most years, in fact, I delay the start of my tench fishing until mid-July, when spawning has been completed.

To some anglers, tench fishing is all about tree-girt lilied ponds, misty dawns, oil-calm water, and needle-bubbles fizzing around a float. All very idyllic – leastways, it is when it's illustrated in a Mr Crabtree comic strip! In reality, such places are smelly, muddy, gnat-infested, claustrophobic, dark, and have an all-pervading sense of decay about them. You can keep them! I'm no lover of estate lakes, either. Reservoirs I could warm to – in fact Ardingly Reservoir, in Sussex, is currently on my 'tench waters to fish' list. For the present, though, I'm a gravel-pit angler through and through, right to the core of my being. Big pits, big sky and big unknown fish – that's my sort of tench fishing!

3 Master Tench Float Fisher

by Keith Sanders

When Bob suggested that I contribute this chapter I was less than enthusiastic. Although I don't still use cane rods, I am at heart a traditionalist, so who in this modern specialist and big-fish-motivated world would be interested in my ramblings? If I was asked what advice I could offer on how to catch bigger tench, my only suggestions would be to concentrate on waters where they lived, and put in the rod hours, which of course is just stating the obvious. Also, I labour when writing, being unable to emulate the methodical composition of the late Len Head, or the enthusiastic eloquence of Chris Yates.

Mr Church, however, is a very persistent fellow and seems to think that a *One Man's Tenching* contribution might even prove interesting. Anyway, a thought came to mind which prompted me to make an effort. This has to do with a trilogy of articles by the late Martin Gay, a good tench angler and writer, although I only knew him from his articles. He outlined his approach to tench fishing and offered some of his thinking relating to 'This beautiful and at times puzzling species': his words. He also suggested there is progress to be made in winter tenching.

It occurred to me that without necessarily attempting to justify the methods I use, if I just write down some recollections of a lifetime spent fishing for tench both winter and summer, it might encourage some small insight into why this beautiful species can at times seem so puzzling.

Having been given honorary membership of the Tenchfishers, I occasionally contribute to the *Tenchfishers'* bulletin. No doubt I will find it necessary to draw on some of those contributions.

If we correctly assume the majority of tench landed each year fall to ledgering methods, mostly linked to audible indicators, then there is little need for concentration; thus the angler may spend time enjoying his surroundings, socializing with other anglers, reading about angling exploits, or just comfortably dozing if so inclined. Then why would anyone contemplate float fishing for them when so much concentration is required to ensure consistent success?

Well, in my case I have never experienced great satisfaction in reeling in self-hooked tench, but I do experience a great adrenalin buzz from converting any indication of a float into a well hooked fish. A purist trout angler might liken it to taking a moderate fish on a dry fly, or a nymph inched slowly across the bottom, as opposed to a double on ledgered lobworm.

WHY USE A FLOAT?

A more practical incentive for float fishing, however, is when tench are at their most vulnerable to ledgering methods, which we know occurs from early spring when they are becoming more active while the natural food source is still scarce. Also angling-induced awareness at this time is at its lowest. This vulnerability can then extend to just after spawning. Even during those weeks when most tench catches are made and most specimens are reported, there will be days when signs of tench activity are very obvious everywhere, with tench rolling and bubbling, but indicators remain motionless.

It is often assumed that a confidently feeding tench will give a confident bite. If bites are twitchy, then they are not feeding confidently. If no bites are forthcoming the assumption may be that they are not interested in what is being offered. But with or without signs of activity, the swim may be wall to wall with tench all going about their normal business of picking up free offerings, yet giving no indication they are feeding.

A not uncommon phenomenon that I have experienced, and which has been recorded by other anglers, is when using a highly visible bait in a swim shallow enough to observe what is happening, and all the free offerings disappear, leaving the hookbait supposedly untouched. Of course, the bait had no doubt been sampled by tench, and may have been taken back to the pharyngeal teeth before the fish possibly sensed the line or braid between their lips and ejected it without the angler being aware. One exception might be if an active worm is used as bait, when the movement of the worm may distract the tench from otherwise sensing something untoward.

I have observed tench tilt down to suck in food, which of course they are obliged to do because they have an upturned mouth, and then not move from that position until they have decided what to retain and what to discard. But if they do not move their body at that moment, there might be no more than a minimal indication to the angler. However, for the second or two that the bait is in the fish's mouth it is potentially catchable, and that is when an ultra-sensitive float set-up can provide success.

'Lay well on, and nail it to the bottom' is a phrase I have often heard from anglers who are float fishing for tench. I accept that this tactic will, on occasion, produce lovely sail-away bites, mostly during those vulnerable weeks, and it is a method I will use if it produces fish. The use of a float ledger can sometimes convert twitches into positive bites.

Some years ago when all forms of ledgering were banned at Sywell reservoir, and only float fishing was allowed, the majority of anglers bent the rules by using a string of triple SSG shot fixed close to a pop-up boilie as bait, together with a Polaris-type sliding self-locking float. Of course little attention was paid to the float. The all-important indicator was the bait-runner reel when a fish hooked itself. This method should not be confused with true float fishing.

It was, I believe, the late Richard Walker who conducted experiments which showed the difficulty in driving a hook home when striking at more than thirty yards using monofilament line, because of the stretch factor. Braid having very little stretch would no doubt extend that distance. So does that mean that probably all fish caught from beyond forty yards are self-hooked?

Sensitivity

Rarely do I use loaded floats, and I will always use as small a float as possible for the prevailing conditions, even down to carrying just one No. 6 shot. Any weight fixed to lie on the bottom is usually less than 6in from the hook.

Inevitably when using short links, the float will then often register what might seem indecisive lifts or dips. This can infuriate some anglers who may assume they are mostly line bites. However, over the years and in every month, winter and summer, I have converted many thousands of these small indications into fish in the net, and this leads me to believe they are the result of tench feeding in a natural and confident manner, as previously described.

Of course I appreciate this method will only appeal to a minority of anglers, and for those who are interested but are not experienced, one very important requirement is to locate tench within a sensitive float-fishing range. If a larger bait such as paste is used, the distance can be extended because it will aid casting and require slightly less sensitivity. Any ledge that is reasonably close in and shelving into deeper water is worth a try.

There is also the need for great concentration, and using more than one rod can be a hindrance. I know my catches over the years would have been far fewer if I had been using two rods. To quote Richard Walker, 'If the fish are feeding, one rod is enough. If they are not feeding, two rods are too many.' Understandably, not everyone has the aptitude for the level of concentration required for longish periods, and also the need to constantly adjust tackle in order to 'fish for bites' as often advised by a great match angler, Ivan Marks.

For some years now my thinking relating to tench fishing has pivoted round the single premise that tench throughout the year mostly do not pick up a bait and move off with it. In my experience the difference between success and failure can be decided by what might seem trivial adjustments such as moving shot slightly up or down, by using different combinations of shotting, even such as substituting two No. 6 in place of one No. 4, or overshotting the float.

The ability to respond in a second to any movement of the float can determine the difference, because that is often the length of time the bait is in the mouth. When I fish, food and drinks are taken with one hand on the rod. If tench are not telepathic, then it is 'Murphy's law' that it will be just at that very moment when probably the only bite of the day occurs. A fast strike can be acquired through practice, and of course it needs to be controlled, especially when using fine lines. The choice of rod is also important.

Colder Months

Usually each year as summer progresses, reports of tench catches to the angling press drop significantly, and any reported after August are often considered as late season, or even cold-water captures. Most anglers then target more obliging species, as tench appear to become less biddable, so although if a mild spell occurs during late autumn, they may become more responsive again for a few days.

For many years now I have concentrated on winter tenching, because for me the satisfaction experienced in landing a tench of perhaps 7lb caught by design in January, far outweighs that in taking a gravid double during the summer months. November into December is usually the least productive time, as water temperature drops until it bottoms out, after which fish may respond to any rise. The lowest water temperature I have recorded with just one tench was 40°F; if it rises to more than 42°F my confidence increases, especially if it remains constant for a few days. During very cold spells I have sometimes refrained from taking the water temperature at all, as it might affect my confidence, so it is possible I have caught at lower than 40°F.

Occasionally tench will indulge in a mini feeding frenzy without necessarily showing a positive indication; I have taken as many as ninety-two tench during one January and February. They feel like ice, but it doesn't affect their performance. However, in my experience, for any sort of consistent success, close location and the use of short links really are a necessity at this time of the year. I also believe, even though I haven't always practised it, that the regular introduction of small amounts of feed into a swim from autumn throughout the coldest months would be beneficial.

On waters where very large amounts of boilies have been continuously introduced and are accepted by the tench as a natural food source, if that feed is continued after autumn, a pop-up anti-eject boilie method might stretch the easy times throughout the winter. This is because if a tench can be persuaded during the colder months to accept a larger bait with a correspondingly larger hook, this has to assist self-hooking. I can remember taking surprising numbers of tench from Sywell reservoir, Northamptonshire, one season during December through to March, using this method – which was, incidentally, to be the last time I would use a bolt rig to catch them. Now the present fashion for carp and tench anglers to feed heavily with much smaller particles makes this less likely.

MY FIRST LIFTS AND LAMPS

More than four decades ago only my summers were spent fishing for tench, as everyone knew that after August they slowly but surely began to hibernate. Autumns and winters were partly spent fishing for chub on the Great Ouse, but mostly for roach on the River Nene. That's when I began to acquire the ability for a fast strike. My rod was a 13ft whole cane with a spliced tip which I had constructed from a kit. It was heavy and out of balance, but the spliced tip helped. My reel was a Grice and Young Royal Avon Supreme Centre Pin. I had to stop using it a few years ago as thumb pressure had worn the rim to a razor-sharp edge; mind you, by that time it had played a great many tench.

The method used for those roach was to fish upstream using stewed wheat as bait, with a shot 1–2in from the hook. The size of shot depended on the strength of flow, and the float was a crow quill with a cork body. Bites were signalled by a slight downstream movement of the float as a roach picked up the bait and moved the shot. That is when I first realized the potential for tench fishing of what is known as the lift method, but used to be known in the 1930s as shot ledgering. I had read of this method being used for tench by the Taylor brothers, but it was my first practical experience of something similar.

There is a stretch of the River Nene near the centre of Northampton known as 'The Leaps'. It is a towpath constructed from bricks and concrete, and is illuminated by street lamps. For some years I would fish for roach during winter evenings from 7pm to 11pm using a lamp to light up a float with an orange tip. This was very successful, with bites being greatly magnified because of water reflection, and it was another method that was to prove very effective in later years when winter tenching.

During those evenings one would meet colourful characters of either gender going about their business. They would often stay for a chat, and the local policeman would enquire whether I had wife trouble (hastily I asserted quite the contrary). Those were good times, and I doubt it would be wise to fish there today, given the many undesirables looking for trouble. A great pity, because it produced some nice roach and chub, and one jet-black tench.

EARLY DAYS AND
MY FIRST TENCH

Now I have a very serious confession regarding my first ever tench. It weighed about 2lb and was caught from a local park lake using worm as bait. Probably I was about ten years old at the time, and as it was during the war years with food rationed, it was triumphantly carried home where it was eaten. Vaguely I remember it tasted rather like eel, but I have prayed for forgiveness ever since.

My teen summers were spent in pursuit of tench at Billing Aquadrome, once the home of big carp, now the caravan Mecca of the Midlands. Those tench were mostly under 3lb, but for each one landed was sown another seed towards an addiction for them.

Then followed a spell serving Queen and country: three years out of five were spent in desert lands. Whilst my comrades were to while away their time fantasizing on the lewder aspects of human behaviour, my dreams were of tree-lined lakes and pools where big tench lived, and all was green. I even acquired a rod made from a tank aerial together with one of the first ambidex fixed-spool reels, and would sit casting to an imaginary bed of lilies in the sand, watching an imaginary float – though only during early morning or late evening, never during the heat of the day. But this behaviour being rather conspicuous, naturally attracted a certain amount of attention, even the odd 'caught anything yet?' Eventually it was adjudged I was 'sand happy'.

One time in Aden I spotted a number of emerald tench near some rocks, and fished for them for hours using various baits, until a sympathetic local informed me they were indeed not tench, but parrot fish, and only fed on coral!

On returning to this green and pleasant land, my obsession was contagious enough to infect an old friend, Lawrie Smith, who became my constant fishing companion. Lawrie has sadly since passed away. We were founder members of the Northampton Specimen Group, we joined the National Association of Specimen Groups, dressed in the right clothes, took water temperatures, and avidly read the writings of the pundits of the day.

Then we purchased Chapman Mk IV cane rods, and new Intrepid Élite reels, the first to incorporate a roller in the bail arm. At last we considered we were well on the way to becoming true specimen hunters. But really tench hunting took precedence over specimen hunting – if they were big, well, that was a bonus. We shared an enthusiasm for catching tench on the float, but resorted to ledgering if conditions dictated.

BOAT FISHING AT
CRANSLEY

Together with another old friend and fellow NSG member, Harold Barrett, we would each summer concentrate on fishing Cransley Reservoir, situated between Northampton and Kettering, a lovely water that has a certain magical quality about it.

In those days Cransley tench grew to 5lb, though they are obviously bigger today. Initially we fished from the bank, which required a good bit of weed dragging, and we did catch quite well; but we felt we could do better, and working on the same old principle 'You only catch fish if you get bites, so fish for bites', that's what we did: instead of waiting for tench to come to us, we went looking for them using a boat. Being mobile, if one spot didn't produce, it was no problem to up anchor and move position.

We sorted the stability problem of float fishing from a boat by using four buckets filled with concrete as anchors. Two were dropped at the rear, often in the margin weed, then after the boat had been quietly moved into position, usually above or in a weedbed such as bistort for cover, the other two buckets were lowered and everything tightened up by pulling and securing the ropes.

Gliding along at first light on the calm surface of a tench water is a really magical experience, and we would often see signs of fish that would be unseen from the bank. At one such time, Lawrie and I spotted some tench rolling among a large bed of giant mare's tail situated at the end and in the middle of one of the arms, growing in 6ft depth of water; I had never seen this particular plant growing at Cransley before. Positioning the boat in the middle of this bed, we carefully lowered the bait: this was either worm or maggot with the float fixed at dead depth and a drilled bullet ledger weight stopped three inches from the hook to ensure the bait had reached the bottom through the weed. Bites were very positive, and we connected with most of them. But playing the fish proved quite spectacular, as the 6lb BS line cut through the stems of the plants and they rose out of the water like enormous lift floats. At the end of the day we had taken about thirty tench and completely decimated the bed of mare's tail. In fact we moved once to find more plants to fish among as we were suddenly in open water and bites had dried up. It never did grow there again.

Our next change of rod happened when a company named Olivers produced a thirteen-foot fibreglass model designed specifically as the first float road for big tench fishing. We christened it 'the totem pole', but being longer it did enable us to have better control, and it did account for a lot of tench, despite the tip dropping abut 12in before responding when striking. Our MK IVs were immediately obsolete as regards tench fishing.

BLOOD AND BRAN

One time we became very excited after reading how Dick Walker and the Taylor brothers had used ox blood to attract tench, because it just so happened Lawrie had access to an abattoir. This was heavy stuff. We would stop en route to Cransley just after the abattoir workers had begun their work, and he would emerge with a container full of the fresh but evil-looking substance. This was added to a bucket containing mashed bread and stiffened up with bran. I remember we all had to help mix this stuff to get the smell on our hands.

It proved fantastic, and although we had little success using it later at Sywell reservoir, at Cransley it reigned supreme. I am convinced it pulled in tench from a great distance. Bait was initially breadflake soaked in blood, but small crust cubes proved better, being more buoyant. Presentation consisted of a single appropriate-size shot fixed no more than two inches from the hook, and a small piece of peacock or crow quill as a float, painted black with a white band up to 1in below the float tip, and set overdepth. After casting, the line was tightened, cocking the float to the shot with the white just under the surface. Bites were signalled by the white suddenly showing, or the float disappearing, and we began to catch many more tench.

Two other friends who were also group members then began to fish Cransley: Jim Haycock and Martin Eckford. They shared the same interest in tench and enjoyed float fishing.

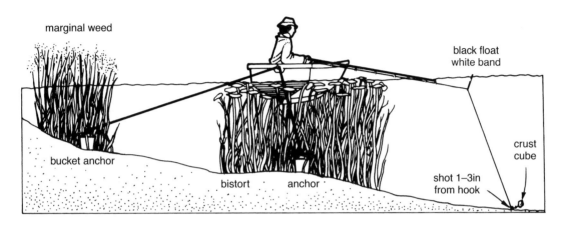

Typical boat position, secured with two anchors at each end. This is the lift method using crust cube bait. The quill float is painted black with a white band.

One boat was bigger, and sometimes there would be three of us fishing from it. When there were just two, we were aware of, and made allowance for, some float movement caused by any movement in the boat. However, with three up, those movements became more unpredictable, and the response to an indication of one's own float was a flick of the eye to see if other floats were behaving in the same way or differently. On occasions three rods would strike in unison with one being connected to a fish. Those sessions usually lasted from 4am until 10pm, and although there was occasional gritting of teeth, no one was ever ejected.

As the weeks progressed the tench became more difficult, and one day we reasoned they were becoming preoccupied with the blood-soaked bran and ignoring the bread. On the next trip, Lawrie and I decided to use no groundbait, and instead threw a length of hosepipe with a brick tied to one end into the swim, and used a funnel to pour diluted blood down the hosepipe. The result was quite spectacular, with a large crimson cloud spreading right across the swim. Within half an hour bites

were so plentiful it seemed we were continually playing fish, and whenever they slowed up it only required a further introduction down the hosepipe to start another feeding frenzy. Incidentally, during the thirty minutes I experimented with a bait lying well on the bottom, only one fish was landed. In those unenlightened days keepnets were common practice and we had tied ours to the back of the boat, until we became fed up with emptying them, and then refilling them again. I honestly don't know how many tench we caught that day. But everything has its price, and disaster struck when our supply of the red stuff was cut off at source. We tried dried blood, but it just didn't work, so we had to start working much harder for our fish.

HEATWAVE TENCH

A day I will always remember was fishing Cransley from the bank with midday temperatures over 90°F and catching thirty-nine tench from just over the marginal weeds in five to six feet depth of water. Large pieces of sausage rusk compressed

65

into a paste were used as bait, moulded on to a size 6 hook. First I introduced three orange-size balls of rusk into the swim, and thereafter bait-size pieces little and often. Occasionally a tench would show itself as it moved up into the margins and then out again, always from left to right. Laying the bait on the bottom produced no interest at all, and the only way I could catch those fish was to suspend the paste bait twelve inches off the bottom underneath an onion-type float. The bites were very positive, so I reasoned the tench were patrolling and just accepted the bait while on the move. This occurred between 8am and 6pm, right through the heat of the day. I knew that fishing on the drop using maggots and casters match-style could be deadly on the day, but this was thumping great lumps of paste. Another valuable lesson learnt.

FIRST EXTENDED FLOAT

It was August and our usual swims at Cransley were proving unproductive. From our observations while in the boat, it appeared that most signs of tench activity had moved to depths of seventeen feet. The use of sliding floats was rejected due to lack of sensitivity, and we decided it needed a fixed-float method. Lawrie and I each purchased a very inexpensive telescopic pole that stretched to twenty-one feet. It may have been before the days of elastic, of which we had no knowledge, so 6lb BS line was tied directly to the pole tip. With this method we did hook a few fish, but it is difficult to describe the experience of having a pole wrapped round and under a boat, or the anchor ropes. The poles were soon discarded and another method had to be found.

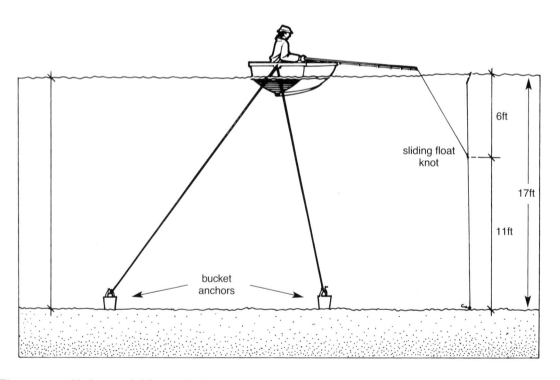

First attempt with the extended float method.

One evening as I was drawing lines on a piece of paper, trying to solve the problem, the answer just seemed to show itself. We called it the extended float method, and it enabled us to fish seventeen feet depths with a fixed float, while using the more powerful thirteen feet 'totem pole'. This did produce some success, but when using it from a boat in that depth we still had problems with the fish getting fouled round the anchor ropes.

The method comprised a six feet length of line fixed to the main line eleven feet above the hook using a sliding float knot so it could be adjusted. The float was attached to the end of the separate piece of line. I doubt we were the first to use this method, and indeed some years later Len Head was to describe it in his excellent book *Tench*. Eventually I found the need to resurrect and fine-tune it to cope with some winter tenching conditions, and that is when its true potential came to be realized.

DALLINGTON

The following introduces a water that provided our first real winter tench success. Near the outskirts of Northampton there is an old estate lake probably still owned by Earl Spencer. At one time, together with some land, it was leased to a tennis club, which also had a subsidiary angling syndicate.

Carp had been introduced in the distant past, obtained I understand from D. F. Leney, who had supplied some of the largest carp to grow in this country. These responded well to the water, and I believe produced a national record before Richard Walker landed his 44lb specimen from Redmire in 1952. Publicity was shunned, but in the early 1960s it contained a number of upper thirties and possibly a forty. Dallington Lake is mentioned in *Confes-sions of a Carp Fisher* by 'BB' (Denys Watkins-Pitchford).

Unfortunately in the bad winter of 1963 a combination of heavy leaf fall and a covering of thick ice for many weeks culminated in the loss of every carp and some other fish. The result was an exodus of members and also of those on the long waiting list. Replacement members were a motley selection, but surprisingly included some enthusiastic tench anglers.

More young carp were obtained, but unlike their predecessors, were destined to reach just low twenties. The surviving tench were quite small, I suppose because of having to compete unsuccessfully with very large carp. It was decided an injection of some reasonable-sized tench was required, and there was Cransley, with what seemed a surplus.

Because of the chance of incrimination, the identity of the anglers involved shall remain anonymous, but if any rules of the day were broken it was in total ignorance.

During a talk with the manager at Cransley, it was revealed that in the archaic rules and conditions for fishing the reservoir, an angler was legally entitled to take away three fish dead or alive at the end of each day's fishing session. This was like a green light. Two buckets complete with lids, each large enough to hold three tench up to 5lb, were obtained. During the following weeks a goodly number of tench over 4lb were successfully introduced into Dallington.

Naturally these activities were observed by other anglers fishing at Cransley, and the manager received a number of complaints that some people were using illegal substances to catch tench, and then selling them to restaurants. The manager requested that these activities be curtailed, and so they were. Of course, in those un-enlightened days the risks involved in moving fish unregulated were unknown by virtually every angler, and such an activity would never have happened today. Luckily no harm was done, and the tench thrived in their new home.

SYWELL

We not only continued to fish Cransley during the summer months, but also Sywell reservoir where Bob Church and friends were catching well, using the feeder method.

During the early years at Sywell, Lawrie, Harold and myself built some portable table platforms which, when placed in the margin reeds, settled in the silt and became quite solid. Wearing waders it was possible to climb on to these and sit on a low chair. We could then fish close to the margins while leaving some reeds in front for cover. These proved successful, but as the feeder method became more popular, with lots of bait going out thirty yards, after the first week or two of the season, many fish moved out to the baited line.

In those days salt could be obtained in block form. By cutting this into smaller cubes and drilling a hole through the centre of each cube, the line some inches above the hook could be looped through the hole and secured with a matchstick. Using this as casting weight which dissolved when wet, it was possible to cast a lightly shotted float and breadflake as bait much further. I remember this method producing sixteen tench in a few hours. It occurred to us then that the salt was probably attracting tench, and possibly the blood used earlier had a saltiness about it. Since then I often use a little sea salt in my paste mixes.

Before becoming a country park, Sywell boasted a big punt-type boat that could be hired for 7s 6d (37½p), and whenever possible we would fish from this. Only once did I attempt to take it out on my own one very foggy morning, and it took me well over two hours to negotiate it into position.

A MILESTONE

Angling Times had printed an article on Cransley tench fishing, and entitled its inhabitants the 'Cransley Tigers' because of their fighting qualities. Sywell tench were on average slightly larger, and because of the weed growth on both waters, we considered 6lb BS line to be the absolute minimum. But each year by late summer tench seemed to stop eating bread, corn, sausage rusk and even maggots, and we then had to content ourselves by turning to other species, such as chub, carp, roach and also barbel – though we had to travel to the River Severn for those.

For roach fishing, Lawrie and I had now acquired a new thirteen-foot glass-fibre match rod, the 'Milbro Enterprise'. While using it one midwinter day I hooked and landed a chub of 3lb plus on 2lb BS line and a size 16 hook. The rod coped very well, and it occurred to me that it might be suitable for taking on hard-fighting tench using balanced tackle, if conditions were right.

The following year, 1976, proved very hot with reservoir levels the lowest for many years, and much less weed. As August slipped by and tench catches tailed off, instead of giving up after a few weeks of blanks, we at last began to use our heads and think things through. It was not feasible that tench were feeding less, so they must be feeding differently, or on much smaller food items, or both. In effect we really had to start fishing for bites.

If we used finer lines it would correspondingly mean much more sensitive float presentation, and balanced with the new rods, a much faster strike. I can remember clearly wondering how these match rods would cope with tench to 5lb. Today I can't believe how naïve we were.

September had arrived, and we decided on Cransley dam for our new venture, using 3lb BS line, two grains of sweetcorn to give a little casting weight and a size 12 hook. It was rare for us to go smaller than a size 10 for tench in those days. Floats were the black-painted quills with the white band, cocked by a single BB shot fixed about 1in from the hook and set one-third overdepth. A small amount of corn with no groundbait was introduced into a seven-foot depth of water.

It was as if a light had suddenly been switched on. We hadn't caught during the previous two weeks, yet on this momentous occasion a milestone occurred that would affect our whole fishing future. With our new striking ability we were hooking and landing a great many tench from the most minuscule of indications, while other anglers who were used to watching 3in of float showing, stood behind us not knowing what we were striking at. The rods performed well, with the reel-setting a little on the light side for the line being used. Actually the reels were the new ABU 444A with the clutch control at the rear, revolutionary at the time, and certainly helpful when playing from the clutch. Later we would often use centrepins.

The wind was blowing from our backs, otherwise it would have been more difficult to detect bites, with presentation much less sensitive, and far fewer fish landed. Since that day I have always contrived to fish without looking into a wind. In my opinion tench are not affected in the same way as carp and bream by wind direction; however, waters can vary. Wind will affect subsurface drift, and this can sometimes be crucial. Tench at one water I used to fish seemed to dislike a strong undertow, and the best spot to locate them was where there was much less underwater movement. Those fish were affected by wind direction. On another pit they would quite happily accept a moving bait fished off the bottom in a strong undertow.

Lawrie and I were now working together, and if we managed to steal away early we could be on Cransley dam by 3pm. One area near the valve tower proved very productive. If we were able to fish from this hot spot, it sometimes happened that whoever managed to cast in first could well be into a fish, and before that was landed the other would also have connected. It was very satisfying fishing and lasted until the water temperature dropped, and we presumed that tench had moved into deeper water.

When it was not possible to offer that sensitive presentation on the reservoir because of unfavourable weather, we moved on to Dallington Lake or a local gravel pit; but we had already greatly extended the tench season.

Winter Speculations

Then more ambitiously we even began to contemplate that consistent tench catches right through the winter might be a possibility. This thought was given greater emphasis after talking with Jim Haycock, a very good friend who had served his apprenticeship in every aspect of angling from a very early age. He has an ability to winkle out tench on days that would seem hopeless to many. This ability extends in the same way to barbel. He was probably the first to discover the now-famous Adams Mill on the Great Ouse, when those barbel were smaller than they are today. Together with a very limited number, we enjoyed the place for a while before an indiscreet word revealed the water to many more anglers, and we stopped fishing there.

But I am digressing. Jim was an instructor in sub-aqua diving, and described how, when taking a party down to test a new underwater searchlight, he had picked out some tench at over 25m depth, where the water temperature was a constant 43°F, being fed from underground springs. They appeared to be moving very slowly and possibly feeding. He did emphasize this was a rather unique water – and he also came across carp at that depth.

During the next two winters we played around with this idea, putting it into practice off and on during milder spells, but with very little success. Location was one big difficulty, as tench would obviously be moving a lot less in low water temperature. Two small ones were taken from Ditchford Gravel Pit, together with some nice roach on corn, but that is a bait I have found to be not very productive in winter. If I were confined to just one single bait for the colder months, it would have to be caster, and a half pint would be enough for three trips. Maggots of course are good, and now I always carry some expander pellets, the sort that need soaking for some hours, then any remaining air forced out of them. Recently I have acquired a pump kit that enables the pellet to be prepared on the bank in minutes using lake water, and also allowing flavour to be added.

THE FIRST REAL WINTER EXPERIENCE

Then one January we heard someone had taken a tench during an afternoon session fishing for roach at Dallington. Suddenly we were focused on something positive. During two consecutive trips fishing from the dam where the depth was about eight feet, we experienced our first real winter success. Five tench, obviously some that had been introduced from Cransley, were landed using fine lines, tiny floats, very little shot and size 16 hooks baited with

maggots. Then all activity stopped for the next two weeks.

While roach fishing the River Nene one evening using a lamp to illuminate a float, I wondered if the same method might work for tench – a possibility we were all interested in. Then Jim and Martin, while walking round Dallington one frosty evening, spotted two tench in shallow water. The most interesting discovery was that the torch did not seem to disturb them. A week later Lawrie and I repeated this experience, the light showing one tench in the shallows, and confirmed it seemed unaffected by the light if moved very slowly; so thereafter, instead of spending winter evenings catching roach, we would focus on tench.

As we had caught from the dam during daylight hours, this seemed to be the obvious place to start. Also it was easier to position the lamps on the level surface of the dam to shine on the floats – which were, of course, fluorescent orange. We did consider it possible that the light might attract fish, although the beam was always aimed across the surface.

That we should have no confidence in baits such as maggots and caster during the hours of darkness seems inexplicable today, but we decided on a more visible bait, breadflake. This produced the occasional indication, none of which we connected with. It was considered that these could be line bites from fish moving up off the bottom, and probably unaware of our baits – as if! Anyway, as an experiment I used one of the new beta lights secured with bands to a short link ledger to draw attention to the bread bait. Astonishingly the float disappeared, and a well-hooked tench was landed. However, it proved too expensive to continue the experiment because the isotope was lost during every strike. I remember Jim also landed a tench using bread after dark.

Finally, sanity prevailed and we did start to use maggots, but the bites were very strange. Exaggerated by the reflection of the float in the water, the tiniest of indications were observed, which it is doubtful would have been noticed in daylight. These would continue for sometimes more than five minutes before a slightly more positive movement resulted in a well-hooked tench. If the float suddenly vanished, it was often less likely that a connection would be made. Also, if the bottom shot was more than a few inches from the hook, bites were rare.

One evening I arrived with Lawrie at about 7pm, and as usual we set up our rods by the headlamps of the car, well away from the lake. Moving down to the dam we threw in some maggots before settling down to fish. Switching on the lamps prior to casting out revealed all the bait on top of a layer of thickening ice! To this day I cannot believe we spent the next hour trying to break a hole in the ice, before retiring defeated.

Winter tench catch in about 1979.

EARLY ENCOUNTER WITH A POSSIBLE SEVEN

At Sywell, it was during the early 1980s that the new species of tench, spawned in the mid-1970s, began to show: young, brilliant-looking, newly mature fish that were already bigger than their predecessors. Immature tench are rarely caught, and it is my belief that any small fish taken regularly are mature, but stunted. Until tench reach maturity and spawn, I don't think they recognize what we throw at them as edible, unless of course it is something natural such as bloodworm. So it was obvious these new fish were the foretaste of something special.

The first experience of just how special was while fishing from the boat with Lawrie. We had settled at over six feet depth, anchored in a bistort bed, and had dragged channels through some milfoil down into deeper water. Using crust cubes on the lift, we had taken about ten or more tench by twitching the bait up the ledge. If a bite happened just after a twitch it was usually very positive, with a fish almost hooking itself, and usually a male. Those older generation tench weighed up to 5lb, while the new, younger specimens were about 5½lb.

Just in front of the boat was a clear area between the bistort and the milfoil. At mid-morning, four tench appeared in this area. We had a few worms, so changing to a larger hook I baited with one. As it settled on the bottom, we watched as they approached the bait. After some minutes, with the tench seemingly undecided what to do with this wriggling object, I recalled an article I had recently read, in which the angler had written how deadly a twitched lobworm was for tench. So I gave it a twitch, and all the tench bolted.

An hour later two more tench arrived, one that we estimated to be about 4½lb, while the other was much larger and could have been 6lb. This time I used a very small worm. The bigger fish approached it, decided it wasn't right and backed off. Suddenly the smaller fish, which hadn't seemed very interested, moved in and the bait disappeared. When landed it weighed 5¾lb, and we then realized that if the larger fish had accepted the bait, it would have been my first seven.

DUSTON MILL PIT

Our fishing almost suffered a double disaster when the water authorities decided to abandon both reservoirs. Cransley was sold off and the fishing became syndicated, while Sywell was offered to Northants County Council for use as a rubbish tip. Happily, after vociferous protests from some local anglers and other concerned parties, the decision was taken to use it as a country park.

We then divided our time between Dallington, Sywell and increasingly a water skirting Northampton which was then known as Duston Mill Pit, but is now known as Sixfields Pit. Today it contains some big carp, and I understand the tench have gained some weight. Although there were always reports of 8lb-plus fish, during the more than twenty years I fished there, I managed to produce just a handful of sixes, and only one 'specimen' that carried a lot of spawn.

This water had proved very interesting, with many features such as reed-lined bays, gravel bars and ledges. There were numerous islands with inaccessible areas, and although Lawrie and I did manage to breach those using our own boat, it made little difference to our catches. From the main bank we had discovered many short-range swims that lent themselves to close-in float fishing, having 7ft depth just off the rod tip, shelving down to 12ft, and often a further ledge shelving again to 17ft.

Today, unfortunately, like many other places, it attracts undesirable elements and crime. But the years I spent fishing there provided me with valuable experience into tench behaviour, especially during the colder months when I found the time slot from 7pm to 10pm quite productive.

One catch that comes to mind was in the year 1981. I know it was that year because I looked it up in *Modern Specimen Hunting* by Jim Gibbinson, in which part of the catch is recorded. I have never kept a diary, and at my age some years become blurred with others. Anyway, this particular winter evening I was using a lamp to illuminate a float, and was fishing in about nine feet depth. Bait was punch bread, together with what was known then as 'rub centre', today described as 'liquidized bread'; in this, the centre of a loaf a few days old was rubbed between the palms of the hand, then compressed gently and thrown into the swim, creating a cloud containing different sized particles. Only small amounts would be used in cold water.

The small piece of bread punch on a size 14 hook produced the familiar tiny indications on the small float. Repeating myself, these would probably not be noticed except that the reflection of the float in the calm surface exaggerated every movement, and which were nearly always preceded, by some minutes, by a more positive indication. To this day, I am perplexed by the cause of those movements, and can only think of tail wash – though that doesn't seem quite right, as tench move much more slowly in colder water. The catch that evening comprised five tench and a chub of 5lb 6oz, the fish mentioned in Jim's book.

A spawny 'specimen' from Duston Mill.

Those winter evening sessions lasted until 1984 when, returning to the car after catching a few tench, I discovered it had been vandalized. In actual fact it had been written off by animal rights activists. In the back of the estate were all my tools of trade, untouched – another sign of how times have changed. Two rods, my Milbro Enterprise, and an Ivan Marks Persuader had been reduced to pieces. On a nearby wall was written an anti-angling slogan.

Now my immediate reaction was not to allow the incident to intimidate me, but as I had been experiencing some eye strain from focusing on an illuminated object for hours at a time, and not wishing any eye problem to jeopardize my daytime float fishing, I decided it was time to stop fishing after dark.

The rod I had been using was a Bob Church 14ft boron with a spliced tip. Later I was to rely on a 13ft Italian carbon rod, the name on it 'Top Tunder Sam'. This has a surprisingly fast response for a rod with a soft action that bends right through to the butt. Today it is still my first choice when using lines of less than 2lb BS, since it absorbs and cushions those jagging lunges tench are capable of performing.

A mid-winter 'after dark' catch using a torch-illuminated float.

TAR AND TENCH

Caster seemed to be the most successful winter bait at Duston Mill, but perch were a problem during daylight hours, although not after dark.

That tench were attracted by the smell of tar was a notion widely held by many angling writers of old, beginning with Isaac Walton. Then I read somewhere that about five decades ago, that a notable and accomplished angler by the name of R. B. Marston claimed to have proved from personal experience that tench were attracted by the odour of tar. He advocated introducing into the groundbait a drop or two of oil of tar. The idea intrigued me, and

A favoured winter swim.

although I personally would never consider using oil of tar, a very unpleasant and poisonous substance liable to burn the skin, I couldn't help but wonder if there was any truth in the theory.

Quite by chance I discovered that the original Fammel cough mixture contained creosote, which of course would be safe to use. Success was instant. We only used it on the hookbait, picking out all the floating casters because of their buoyancy, and soaking them in water containing a few drops of the mixture. There were no more problems with perch, but the tench certainly homed in on the scent emitting from that one particle, and the difference between flavoured and unflavoured caster was unmistakable. Unfortunately the manufacturers, in their wisdom, then improved the recipe, and it stopped working for us. I have searched for, and tried some alternatives, but without success. Since then I have always washed my hands in Wrights Coal Tar Soap before every fishing trip.

Famell-flavoured casters produced this winter catch.

EXPERIENCES WITH PREOCCUPATION

A few years later in early January, during a spell of mild weather, with water temperatures moving from 41°F to 43°F, I had actually intended a rare trip for barbel on the Great Ouse. The hemp had been prepared the previous day – *but* I had failed to stay in touch with the weather forecast, and the day dawned with a cold north-easterly blowing. Well, there was no way I was going to sit on a river bank looking that in the face. The temperature in my garden pond still showed 43°F, so it was decided to head instead for the pit swim, which offered good protection from that wind. Barbel tackle was unloaded, and replaced with the soft Italian rod and centrepin loaded with 2½lb BS Ultima. There were casters for

bait, and I also decided to take the hemp, something I had not used before for winter tench.

The walk to the swim is over rough high ground, and even with the cutting wind I began to perspire inside the Bob Church suit and thermal boots. On descending to water level through quickthorn and briars, peaceful calm replaced the cold wind, and with the sun out, some minutes were spent ventilating while surveying the calm water.

Water temperature was confirmed by the thermometer as still 43°F. This spot really consists of two swims, the one I intended to fish, and another round a bend to the right more suited to an easterly wind; a gravel bar separates the two. On impulse, three good handfuls of hemp were thrown into each swim, and I proceeded to fish using caster as bait.

Tackle consisted of a size 18 Drennan carbon spade hook tied to 1.7lb BS Ultima bottom. The float was a canal grey carrying two No. 4 shot, into which was inserted ¼in of nylon bristle; this was used with just the bristle showing. After two hours without a bite, a move was made to the swim on the right. Another hour passed with no sign of a bite, and I wondered what had possessed me throwing in all that hemp and probably ruining both swims.

Suddenly I felt compelled to look again at the other swim. Walking slowly along the bank I could hardly believe my eyes when seeing a sight I had never seen before or since in mid-winter. The surface over the baited area was covered in tench blows, tiny frothy bubbles that slowly drifted away, and more appeared as if by magic. My mouth gaped for some minutes before I managed to co-ordinate my senses; then I returned my tackle to the swim and started to fish with trembling hands.

This swim had a bank-side depth of 5ft shelving to 7ft, then a ledge of 18in just off the rod tip, and shelving again to 12ft or more. The baited area was on and just beyond the ledge.

Another hour of hard fishing using various permutations of caster direct-hooked and hair-rigged, flavoured with the cough mixture, and also with a hemp flavour, was all in vain – and still the blows continued. Then it suddenly dawned on me what was amiss, and I did what I should have done an hour earlier: threaded three grains of hemp on to a hair tied to the size 18 hook. When fishing under the rod top, and hair-rigging lightweight baits such as hemp or caster, the bait is threaded on to the hair made from 8oz BS line using a fine needle, and held in place by a knot tied in the hair.

It still took another thirty minutes to get the presentation right. The small bristle was showing nothing really, just a feeling I had seen something, but not enough to strike at. The float was therefore changed to one similar, but without the bristle. This was presented with the bait an inch or two up the ledge, and just ¹⁄₁₆in of black float tip

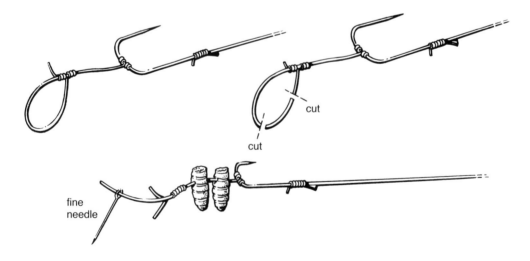

Hair rig using 8oz BS line for caster or hemp at close range.

showing, overshotted by a No. 8 shot 3in from the hook.

The first positive bite was missed, a slight flattening of the tiny dot. While rebaiting and casting I had difficulty in breathing until the arm responded to the eye, the soft rod curved over, and at last I experienced the satisfaction of feeling the centrepin giving line under thumb pressure. With tackle nicely balanced the fine line is adequate, and a tench just under 5lb in peak condition was landed.

The rest of the day until nearly dusk produced another twelve tench to a little over 5lb; two were lost when the hook pulled out, possibly foul hooked, and a few bites were missed. Having cracked the fishing for the day, it had suddenly become easy, and I was glad to stop. The sun had gone down and the air was very chilled, but those tench were still blowing when I left.

The same swim was fished two days later. The water temperature had dropped to 41°F, and caster produced one bite that was missed. I thought I had really cracked it, but since then hemp has not yielded another winter tench, and is no longer included in my permutations. This was one of many experiences that helped lead me to believe that no conclusion regarding tench fishing should be set in stone; it was just one example of tench preoccupation with a particular small food item to the exclusion of all else.

Many anglers experience success by baiting a swim heavily with a mixture of small particles, and sitting on it for possibly a number of days waiting for the tench to arrive and begin to feed over it. In my experience that tactic does not lend itself very often to fishing short sessions, and if I can locate tench it becomes unnecessary. One rule I nearly always observe now is, if I can't put it on a hook or a hair, I don't throw it in, and only on rare occasions do I use groundbait.

Winter hemp swim; the Italian rod in action.

I recall another example of preoccupation on a gravel pit where the tench just loved golden crumb. They would continue to move over a baited area until every last crumb had been hoovered up, and every other food item put in with it ignored – at least, it was if it was attached to a hook! Crumb used as paste produced no bites, even though the whole surface area where the groundbait lay was a cauldron of fizzy blows.

The problem was resolved using Rice Crispies. When placed on top of a small amount of damp crumb, the texture became soft, but with enough substance to allow two or three Crispies be put on a small hook. They also took on the colour of the crumb.

A nice winter tench and a familiar Northampton landmark.

On another occasion I was fishing one February day with friends Jim and Martin at one of our favourite spots on the pit. Martin was fishing in the middle with Jim on his left, each of us using caster without success. Then in the early afternoon for just a couple of hours, Martin landed a few tench from very positive bites after hair-rigging large pieces of paste with three casters on the hook; we remained biteless. He was using a very prominent float, while ours were dotted right down.

Rather than let this occurrence undermine our hard-won experience regarding winter tench, Jim and I decided the paste must be acting as a bolt rig and those fish were hooking themselves. But of course it might also have been the result of their being offered something quite different.

RESURRECTED

It was while winter fishing Duston Mill that the extended float method was resurrected because, once again, we wanted to experiment in depths greater than the rod length. Now although these depths have produced some tench in the colder months, I have found that waters under 11ft in depth were more productive than those that were over 11ft. At Sywell, fishing depths between 5ft and 8ft on the west arm proved quite successful one winter, while during that same period the dam also produced fish at depths up to 17ft. The only conclusion that might be reached from these experiences is that tench don't always retire to the deepest water in winter.

However, having looked again at the method, its full potential was soon perceived, because not only was it useful for deep water, it was also perfect for beating strong surface drifts, with line sunk so deep. And although it could still be affected by undertows, bite connection was

The first time I used this bait it accounted for twenty-three tench including one recognizable male that was landed twice. The successful method was a tiny crow quill cocked by a No. 6 shot and placed 2ft from the hook, with the bait just off or just on the bottom. If a less sensitive float was used, or any shot on the bottom, bites were much less decisive. However, as long as the groundbait kept going in, bites kept coming. An unsuccessful angler fishing opposite called across asking what I was using. When told, his reply was 'Pull the other one!', or words to that effect. And after four weeks those tench were eating golden crumb much less confidently.

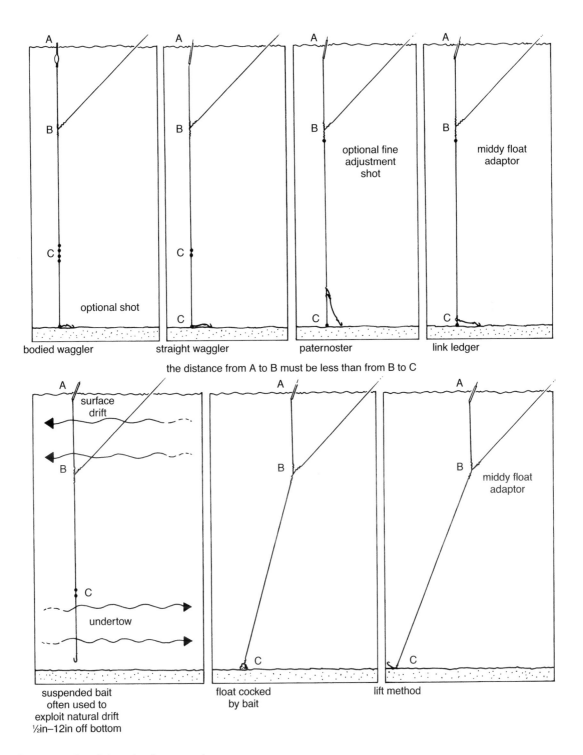

bodied waggler straight waggler paternoster link ledger

optional fine adjustment shot

middy float adaptor

optional shot

the distance from A to B must be less than from B to C

surface drift

undertow

suspended bait often used to exploit natural drift ½in–12in off bottom

float cocked by bait

lift method

middy float adaptor

Some examples of rigs using float extensions.

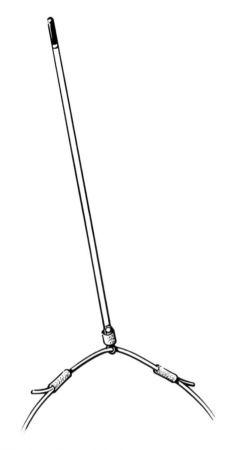

Middy float adaptor with silicone tube and nylon bristle stops.

having the float cocked by just the bait with no other weight added. A boilie-size piece of paste and a peacock-quill float can be cast 30yd, offering the perfect lift method. It is, however, important to remember two rules when using this method to allow successful casting and to avoid tangles. Firstly the line used for the extension should not be too fine. 5lb BS is about right. The other rule is that the length of mainline from the attachment point to any bulk weight added should be greater than the length of the extension line including the float.

One item of tackle I would be loathe to fish without costs only a few pence: a middy quick-change float adaptor. With this I can change a float in seconds. To fix it in position I use short lengths of silicone tubing with nylon bristles inserted, one above the adaptor, one below. This allows fast adjustment of depth. Also with no shot required to lock the float it helps towards greater versatility, such as when the lift method is used, placing all the weight where it does the most good, close to the bait and nowhere near the float. If the requirement is to combat drift, the full buoyancy of the float is allowed to work. It is also line friendly.

When using the extended float method, if a loop is tied to each end of the extension line, one of these can be easily attached to the float adaptor, and the other pushed through the float eye, then looped over the top of the float and pulled down to secure it. Like this, change of presentation or method can be accomplished fast and easily.

HOTSPOTS

Having stressed a number of times how close location can be all important, perhaps I should describe how often we found

improved as the main line was more direct to the bait. Also it allowed a much smaller float to be used than conditions would normally dictate.

The minimum depth at which this method is practical is about 4ft, with a 12in extension for the float. I have used it successfully in 6ft of water with the bait off the bottom moving at the correct speed in an undertow, whereas the float would normally have been pushed in the opposite direction by the wind and surface drift, spoiling the presentation.

At Sywell I have found it invaluable, none more so than when using paste and just a few yards to be crucial. When fishing from a boat, usually just the length of the boat separated our baits. On quite a number of occasions over the years, one end of the boat would produce tench, while there was no sign of activity for the poor unfortunate sitting at the other end.

Sometimes if we changed places, it would reveal a small difference in presentation, and when corrected all would be well. But more often it confirmed the presence of tench in that one spot, while the rest of what in effect was just one big swim, seemed devoid of fish.

Another example occurred after spending 16 June in hospital due to the removal of a malignant melanoma from my left leg, which resulted in a skin graft, and being sent home to spend many weeks with my leg in plaster from ankle to thigh. My friends rallied round and would take turns ferrying me to Sywell, where I would sit with my plastered leg resting on an upturned bucket.

One such day found Harold and myself fishing just a few yards apart near the oaks on the east bank. Harold had been catching well all morning, while I remained biteless. At midday he had to leave for a couple of hours, during which time I was sorely tempted to cast into his swim. This I resisted, thinking that, if Harold was not there to intercept every tench, which in my mind must have been moving from left to right, I would eventually catch from the spot I was fishing. But I didn't. On his return he cast out and promptly connected to another tench. We were both using the same bait, and the same float method. No weedbed or feature separated our baits.

As a consequence of many experiences of that kind, I now systematically explore every part of a swim, and very often there will be a hotspot somewhere, even though loose feed might be spread right across the area. Success in the past has sometimes been achieved after moving swims up to two or even three times in a day looking for tench.

NODDY FISHING AT TC PIT

As mentioned earlier I have never kept a real record of all my years spent fishing, but it was the early 1980s when I first visited the T.C. Pit near Oxford. I knew that some big tench catches had been made from there for a number of years by Tony Miles, Trevor West and a little later by another very good angler, Alan Smith. I heard it was receiving heavy pressure and the tench became difficult after the first few weeks of a season.

My first trip was in August, and was just a look-see really. Alan had explained where I could find some reasonable depth close in, so I didn't have to do any work. In three hours I landed three tench to 6½lb on sweetcorn using the lift method. This did sharpen my appetite, and although I only managed two more trips that year, over the next few years I experienced some very enjoyable day sessions there. For anyone who knows the water, I concentrated on the canal and river banks.

One such very hot, sunny, mid-August day I was fishing from the canal bank. Bait was sweetcorn and caster, and had been liberally scattered about in seven feet of water at dawn. The swim had been dragged by myself earlier in the season, and presumably by others since, as it was possible to twitch a bait through without picking up any debris on the hook.

One tench was landed at 7.30am on corn, and another an hour later on caster. Both were positive bites and probably any method within reason would have caught those fish. Another hour passed, no more bites materialized, and many anglers would have decided that sport had ceased through the heat of the day, with not a breath of wind.

Going on past experience, I always assume that for every tench that gives a positive bite, there could be many more in the swim that will not. Changing down to a lighter line was out of the question, and the 5lb BS line was as fine as could be risked because of weed growth.

After trying various presentations that would show easy bites, I began to connect with fish again using the familiar black crow quill with the white band ½in below the tip. This was balanced to a single shot 1in from a size 16 hook and fished 3ft overdepth. Bait was two black, very buoyant casters on the hook, and as bites tailed off, I began to catch again using a hair. At about midday with the sun high and very hot, bites ceased. One black and two light-coloured casters on a hair accounted for a nice tench of 7lb 3oz, and then nothing again. They obviously wanted the light-coloured casters, but the combined weight of bait and hook proved suspiciously heavy. Finally I was reduced to the ridiculous situation of snipping off the tip of one of the casters and inserting a tiny polystyrene ball. Today I would have used one of the buoyant imitations. This, however, was accepted again, and by late afternoon more than twenty tench to over 7lb had been landed. Only rarely was the bite indicated by the float going under, and never by its lying flat. On that day, if the shot had been more than 1in from the hook, it would have been a waste of time fishing.

Two anglers had spent some days (and nights) in the swim from which Alan Smith had caught his then record bream, and from which the late Alan Wilson subsequently landed a record catch of double-figure bream. They walked around and peered over the brambles behind me, and one remarked to the other: 'It's only a – noddy.' Float angling was derided in those days by some 'specimen hunters' as noddy fishing.

I remember thinking, that's OK, the more people that cast to the horizon, the less crowded the margins will be.

IRISH CANAL TENCH

The year 1986 stands out in my memory. During a week spent tench fishing in Ireland with Jim, one day proved very educational. We had experienced meagre results near Carrick-on-Shannon, so decided to leave early on the last day to try our luck on a stretch of canal that the locals insisted was full of tench. Because there was no boat traffic on this section it was crystal clear and full of marestail, together with some broad-leafed pondweed. After leaving the car, we walked about five hundred yards along the overgrown towpath without a sign of fish, until suddenly we spotted a tench moving across one of the clear spots.

Before tackling up, I threw in a small amount of groundbait, corn and caster into a weed-free area. A number of tench emerged from the surrounding weed, consumed the feed, and disappeared before I had cast in. With my bait – a single grain of corn – in position, I once again introduced some loose feed, and once again the tench repeated their previous behaviour, leaving my float seemingly untroubled. This occurred a number of times, during which I tried various presentations before a slight lifting of the float while using caster caused me to strike. This resulted in a pricked fish that was on for just a second (it may have been foul-hooked), whereupon all the tench vanished into the weed. At the end of the day the remaining groundbait was still visible because those fish did not return to feed again in that spot.

Jim was using the lift method, and we watched with interest as a tench sucked in his single corn bait without moving the shot that was just a couple of inches from the hook. After some seconds it ejected it, without the float showing the slightest indication.

Eventually we were rewarded after clearing some holes in the weed using a small scythe that screwed into a landing-net pole. These holes were baited, and if after half an hour the bait had gone, we were in business. One method that produced results was to use caster just off the bottom and strike at anything. After connecting once, no more bites would be forthcoming from that swim, and a move was required.

The experience gained that one day proved invaluable to both of us. As the water was virtually unfished, angling pressure could not be blamed for the behaviour of those tench. It was a fascinating visual confirmation of normal tench behaviour.

DISCOVERING HOLLOWELL

Another reason for remembering 1986 was Hollowell Reservoir. Although it is situated just twenty minutes from my home, I had never fished there. It was not then known as a tench water, though was well known by Midlands match anglers for its roach hybrids.

Early that season I had visited a local tackle shop and overheard someone mention seeing a tench roll while fishing there. This sounded interesting, and after meeting Jim we spent that evening walking right round the reservoir. Just as we were crossing the dam to return to the car, I spotted a good tench roll. Jim didn't see this, which was a pity, because if he had, I know he would have been more enthusiastic.

The next day I visited again, armed with a rod, bait and my usual drag made from two rake heads back to back. After checking the depth off the dam near where I had

seen the tench, I threw in the drag, which promptly became firmly lodged in the uneven stones with which the dam wall is constructed. That evening I returned with a new drag made from a piece of hardwood with sheet lead and barbed wire wrapped round it. This worked very well, and I cleared pondweed, milfoil and also some filamentous algae that covered the bottom for some inches in height. Mashed bread and a can of sweetcorn were then introduced.

As I drove to the reservoir early the following morning, it was with that great feeling of eager anticipation that can accompany fishing a new water for the first time. An overcast sky together with a light-to-moderate easterly wind chilled the air a little as I set up in the prepared swim. Thankfully I had had the foresight to place a mark on the featureless dam.

The rod I was using at that time was an Excalibur Quiver feeder rod, not designed for float fishing, but it proved very successful. With the push-in quiver fitted it allowed for a reasonably fast strike, while the rod provided a lot of power.

Because of the algae, I decided to use no shot on the bottom, hoping the bait would not sink out of sight. Two grains of corn on a size 12 Drennan specimen hook combined with a Drennan 4 No. 4 fine-insert crystal float produced a bite within minutes of the first cast: just a slight dip, and such was my surprise that I made no attempt to strike. Ten minutes later, with no further indication, I retrieved, and before rebaiting scooped out the kernel from one piece of corn and inserted a tiny polystyrene ball, hoping for almost neutral buoyancy of the bait. Once again, today I would have used a buoyant imitation.

The next bite was more positive, and the resulting strike connected to something bigger than I had ever previously experienced. It was played with great care, and

The first Hollowell tench, at 9lb 13oz.

netted with great relief. My first Hollowell tench, and my first nine at 9lb 13oz. I remember thinking, this must be a magical place, this is the stuff of fairy stories...

An hour later, and I had not had another bite from that spot, just over two rod-lengths out. Meanwhile I had been baiting with corn and caster in a line from that point to just off the sunken rod tip, over which a tench suddenly rolled. It still surprises me slightly even after years of such experiences, how close a tench will roll to where I am sitting; they often move right close in to the margins, but just out of vision even when using polaroids, probably in about six feet depth.

Hurriedly I lowered the float, baited with three casters, and positioned the bait with the float just a few feet from the rod top. A few minutes later the float buried and a tench of about 6½lb was landed.

At that point I returned to the car for a keepnet, into which another nine tench were retained, all taken on caster. The reason I had left the net behind was a half-hearted decision to stop using one. In actual fact that was the last time I did retain any fish, instead I invested in a camera with a timer.

As there was no one in the vicinity the big one was photographed on the ground using a small compact I had been given, but rarely used. It had never seemed an important issue to record my catches, although I did feel obliged to present some of them to the group for their records. From memory I believe the rest of the catch consisted of two eights, and some sevens and sixes.

Those fish were witnessed by just one person, but within days well-known anglers were arriving from all over. Three weeks later the angling press tracked me down after printing rumours of a big tench catch, pointing out it was every angler's duty to report such catches.

Those tench continued to feed through the summer, and I continued to catch. No one else seemed to have much success though, probably because psychologically few could really accept fishing so close on such a large water. Some years later the reason for those tench being there revealed itself. At intervals the gaps in the stones on the dam had been infilled with gravel. Over the years this had been washed down by rain into the reservoir, and had created a gravel path about 2ft wide in 5ft to 6ft depths of water on which the algae did not grow. This was a natural patrol route, and any bait presented there was more visible to the tench. The first fish landed was probably the result of bait dropping where the algae had been disturbed by my dragging. At Hollowell it is only when the filamentous algae grows prolifically on the dam that any numbers of tench are attracted to within float-fishing range. The years between this happening I leave to the long-range anglers, because today Hollowell is a well-known big tench water.

MY FIRST DOUBLE

During the rest of the 1980s and into the 1990s, a great many tench were taken by a great many anglers at Sywell, mostly to boilies, but occasionally on maggot or corn in the first few weeks of some seasons. Anglers arrived from all parts of the country, and having invested much effort and cost into the venture, naturally desired a return on that investment, which for most meant landing a personal best. Reports in the angling press of the day almost guaranteed this would happen. Sadly I met people complaining of only landing spawny sevens instead of a spawny eight, which consequently meant the venture had been a failure and they were most dejected. Some obviously believed a big fish was needed to boost their standing in the eyes of their peers, a fundamental doctrine that can be traced back to the emergence of specimen groups, when the illusion was perpetuated that an angler who caught a better-than-average fish was automatically elevated to a better-than-average angler. And we all went looking for personal bests. I am reminded now of collecting train numbers as children, and boasting if we had seen something special.

One evening I landed four tench over 8lb on float-fished caster, but I know skill did not determine the size of fish that picked up my bait; that was more down to the fact that I live just twenty minutes from Sywell. My first double at 10lb 1oz came from Sywell dam. Alan Smith had mentioned that while carp fishing using tiger nuts he had observed some tench feeding on them. At that time there was some doubt about the ability of fish to digest them because of their hardness, regardless of how long they had been soaked or prepared. The tigers put into my garden pond were easily dealt with: I watched a golden orfe of 5lb take one in, and within a few seconds blow out the debris. I would suggest the attraction is in the oil content.

Four weeks before the season started I began to introduce them all along the dam. It was two weeks into the season, and although I had been using them for a while each session, there was no sign of interest.

During one very wet day a few average tench had been taken on paste, and as I

Sywell 9lb 15oz sausage-meat paste; the lift method.

always play a hooked fish well away from the swim if possible, I was getting rather wet. Sitting under the umbrella drinking a cup of coffee, I had baited with a tiger, not expecting a bite and thinking that I would be able to enjoy my drink in peace. So when the float vanished it came as a complete surprise, and my coffee cup was in the wrong hand. Recasting and fully prepared when the float indicated the next bite, I connected and netted another personal best. The method used to take that fish and two subsequent tench, each about 8lb (although I didn't weigh them), consisted of a small quill float and no shot on the bottom, just 1 BB fixed at half the 8ft depth, which, combined with the bait, would have sunk the float. Now the only skill required to hook that double was an ability to catch tench, though in fact all other bites I experienced before I had to leave were missed.

The next day I returned with enough confidence to use only tiger nuts as bait. Using the same presentation, I once again began to miss very positive bites, and it was only when, in desperation, I laid the bait and shot well on the bottom that I began to hook some nice roach up to just under 2lb. They were the only tench to fall to tigers. However, having bought a sackful following a bad harvest when they were expensive, I decided to find out if barbel liked them. After pre-baiting at Harold on the Great Ouse, they accounted for just one barbel – but the chub almost crawled up the rod for them.

LIFE AFTER THE BAN AT SYWELL

By the early 1990s there were increasing signs of the considerable angling pressure on the tench at Sywell. Stepped-up carp tackle together with bolt-rig weights up to 3oz were being used by a majority of people, and cast well beyond thirty yards of dense beds of weed.

Roy Westwood, then editor of *Anglers Mail*, wrote in his 'End Peg Column' some years later the following words, which summarized exactly the situation as it had developed:

The Canadian pondweed has now died back and slumped to the bottom at Sywell Reservoir in Northamptonshire. But it will surely explode into life again next spring and throttle the tench haven.

Chemical treatment is impossible and in cases of extreme infestation like Sywell, anglers must adapt to the challenge of the underwater jungle or fish elsewhere.

In past seasons, some responded by dragging out the tench with beachcaster tackle. Inevitably, the fish became disfigured, sad caricatures of their species as the heavy bombs and line took their toll.

Astonishingly, many Sywell anglers appeared to accept this mouth and fin damage as an inevitable consequence of the heavy growths of pondweed. They appeared to blame photosynthesis, and not themselves!

When the ledger ban, originally initiated by the controlling club, was imposed, I was publicly involved and of course it was very controversial. It was remarked that overnight I became less popular than a cormorant, and my wife and I well remember the threatening telephone calls.

As the number of anglers fishing Sywell became fewer, the club, worried about the loss of revenue, asked me to offer some advice to anglers not used to float fishing such waters for tench. The following was printed in their newsletter:

An article in a monthly magazine posed the question: 'Is there life after the ban at Sywell?' The author was optimistic, and he was right to be so.

The fishing has been good for those anglers willing to learn new skills, or rediscover old ones. This, despite the water level being some feet below normal, making many swims very messy with up to a foot of silt exposed. For any angler who feels that float fishing at Sywell is a daunting proposition, let me assure them that it can be relatively easy, providing it is approached in the right frame of mind.

Firstly ignore all tench rolling more than thirty yards out; it only leads to frustration if you don't, and there are plenty to be caught within that distance. Always carry a drag (no swim is unfishable, despite weed density) and use it! It will not frighten the tench, more likely the disturbance will attract them. Forget about missile-type floats with a string of swan shot in an attempt to imitate the bolt rig. Drennon peacock floats 6in to 10in will be suitable for most conditions. Tie 6lb to 8lb line to a size 8 specimen hook (barbless), leaving the loose end 1in long as a hair, fit on a ledger stop to mould on a paste bait, and use the bait for casting weight. Boilie-size baits will cast up to thirty yards if needed. Only use shot to secure the float, but leave it undershotted and fished overdepth. After casting, sink the line and tighten up to the bait until the float cocks. A black float works well, and you should strike when it disappears or lies flat. It does require concentration, and using two rods can be counter productive. I know some anglers can feel disadvantaged using only one rod, but there are days when many bites are missed while waiting for one of a pair of totem pole floats to vanish.

To date, I have landed 264 tench since June 16th this year, with over half of them being taken from areas other than the dam wall. The largest, 8lb 14oz, came from the oaks swim. The most productive day accounted for twenty-three fish from one of the swims furthest from the car park. Most were taken on the method described above. A more recent catch in October comprised nine tench between 6lb and 8lb using a sliding float and maggot as hookbait, and fellow angler Jim Haycock landed two fish, both eights. Sywell finished? I don't think so.

Anglers should escape from the tunnel vision of optonics, self-hooking rigs, and casting to the horizon. Give float fishing a chance: you never know, you may even enjoy it. Most importantly, there are now very visible signs that the ledger ban has been justified. The real winners are the tench, and that is something I can live with.

The last few words proved prophetic. Although few anglers took my words of wisdom 'on board', angling pressure was greatly reduced for a number of years, giving those tench enough time to recover. A few battle-scarred veterans have survived, but the quality of Sywell tench today is truly superb, with fish to 12lb plus.

Bill Hutchinson of Tek-Neek, who now controls the fishing, has reintroduced ledgering, limiting weights to 1oz only, and no fixed ledger weights, among other sensible rules.

A DOUBLE FROM A FLAT CALM

At present I often use Drennan tench float rods; there may be better rods out there, but these do all I ask of them, even short distance, light ledger work on the rare occasion. Each of their three models has a slightly different action. I have only one small criticism, concerning the traditional reel fittings that Drennan insist on using: the centrepin kept dropping off, so I've had mine modified with screw fittings.

When I mention the size of floats I use, especially on reservoirs, some people are sceptical. Many anglers who firmly believe the only place to catch tench is facing the wind, are uncomfortable fishing on a flat-calm water. However, I get away with using my small floats by seeking out such places; even in the most adverse conditions there is usually somewhere much less affected. As mentioned earlier, in my experience I have never found it necessary to fish into the wind to catch tench.

Shown is a picture of a 10lb 6oz fish taken from Sywell. For those familiar with the water, it came from the east arm looking towards the main east bank. That day a very brisk north-westerly was blowing, white horses were breaking against the

*A Sywell 10lb 6oz
fish from a flat calm.*

dam, and the oaks area just visible on the left of the picture was pretty rough. But I had high ground and the wind behind me, and it was a very different world.

The first hour was spent dragging to a depth of 7ft. I was fishing by 9am, tench began to show interest at about 11am, and by 4pm I had taken this fish and several others, all over 7lb, using 6in of peacock float cocked by a piece of hair-rigged paste flavoured with solar squid and octopus. The big one was landed at 2pm, another personal best, thanks to Lady Luck.

GRENDON LAKES

In recent years I increasingly have problems walking any distance from the car, even when using a trolley for carrying tackle. At the reservoirs the dam walls are now my only viable option on days that are windless, or blowing from a southerly direction. I often fish at a complex of gravel pits where the car may be driven close to many swims. Grendon Lakes contain biggish carp reported to 42lb, bream to 13lb, and tench just into doubles, but mostly between 4½lb and 6½lb. It has proved a very useful winter tench venue with depths to 16ft. During the summer months it has produced for me twenty-plus tench in a few hours.

Earlier I mentioned how in my experience, success or failure can often be decided by what might seem trivial adjustments. One presentation I often use can sometimes determine whether tench are

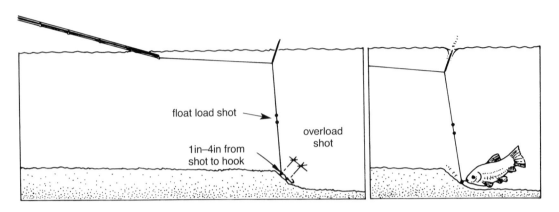

Overload method on a ledge. As a fish picks up the bait, the overload shot falls down the ledge taking the float under.

present in a swim, when previously it has seemed devoid of fish. For this to work effectively a ledge is required in a swim, on which a bait can be placed. Overload a small float with a shot fixed up to 3in from the hook, and position the bait down the ledge at various depths, searching for bites. When the bait is sampled, the shot is disturbed, causing it to fall down the ledge, and even if the shot is lifted, the effect is usually the same, namely the float goes under. This can sometimes produce a lot of fish, though often the bait has been ejected before the indication registers. However, it provides something tangible to work on.

I remember one occasion when this method worked well: I had arrived at mid-morning to find the pit had been booked for a match, which by then was in full progress. Every participant was using either the Method or feeder, with what seemed a considerable financial outlay in bait. Very few fish were caught, and the match was won with just two fish.

After assuring the match organizer I was only going to float fish off the rod tip, I was given permission to settle in a vacant area where there was a ledge dropping from 5ft to 8ft, and the surface was a flat calm. I had

recently acquired a 17ft Daiwa match carp rod that was proving very successful (it would subsequently account for a 10lb 8oz fish from Hollowell), and my only bait was Tesco's (good value/minimal cost) baked beans. A particle bait which I have found requires very little, if any, prebaiting, but is only suitable for close-in fishing because of its softness.

For twenty minutes I tried normal laying on, with the bottom shot 8in from the hook, and using a 2 No. 4 fine-insert crystal float. With no sign of interest I moved the shot to half depth, then took an extra No. 4 and placed it 3in from the bait, which was precisely positioned just down the ledge with 1in of float showing. The response was instant, with the float shooting under very fast. This was repeated every cast, all of which were missed, retrieving only the skin of the bean. After moving the shot a little closer to the hook and sinking the float until ¼in showed, my reactions were just fast enough to connect with about one in four bites, mostly hooked inside the scissors. Losing count of the number of times I walked along the bank carrying a fish-laden net to release them away from the spot I was

A Hollowell tench at 10lb 13oz. Note the cyst.

fishing, I suddenly became aware of many eyes in my direction, accompanied by much muttering. Actually I stopped fishing before the match finished, in some embarrassment.

The really sad thing, however, was that not one of those match anglers set up a float rod. Those tench were in the swim and feeding well, but if I had not used that specific method, I might have been totally unaware of their presence.

MORE SUCCESS AT HOLLOWELL

It was summer 2001 when a friend, Bob Graves, who is also a good tench float angler, telephoned me to say that foot and mouth restrictions had been lifted at Hollowell, but only the dam wall could be fished. Not only was the filamentous algae growing prolifically on the dam, but he had landed a tench of 11lb on float-fished corn. The following day I purchased a season ticket and was fishing by 11am. Bob had been there for some hours, and had landed four tench.

By the time I arrived the wind had increased, making sensitive float presentation difficult, and at 1pm I discarded the float in favour of a running ledger. Then I tried a paternoster set-up with varying lengths of tail; when using a very short

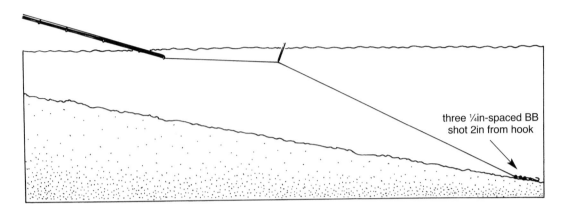

three ¼in-spaced BB
shot 2in from hook

The method used to take the 10lb 13oz fish: a self-cocking float is used as a slider without a stop.

hook-link the small bobbin indicator flicked occasionally. Some may have considered these to be line bites, but I was convinced that these indications were caused by tench picking up the bait but rejecting it instantly.

An hour later I went back to a small self-cocking float that didn't quite carry an extra three BB. The bottom shot was placed about 2in from the hook, with ¼in space between each of the three shot. It only required a movement of the first shot to register something. Bait was a piece of corn, together with a buoyant imitation on a short hair tied to a size 10 hook.

After casting, the float, which was used as a slider without a stop, was allowed to run up the line until it balanced in the drift a few feet from the submerged rod top, with about 1in of black tip showing. A few minutes later the float lifted slightly, and if my hand had not been on the rod I would have missed it. As it was, I experienced an adrenalin rush augmented by the sound of line singing in the wind. When the fish surfaced for a second, I knew she was special, but my uppermost thought was 'please don't let it be Bob's eleven!' Well, she

wasn't, and she weighed 10lb 13oz and was in superb condition. Incidentally, as long as Hollowell does not contain two doubles with a cyst near the mouth, then this fish and I have since renewed our acquaintance.

The line that day was 5lb BS Super Shinobi. When using hair rigs I find that Drennan specimen eyed barbless work well enough; for most everything else I now use Preston PR21 spade barbless, which are not made from the heaviest wire but are strong and have a wide gape, perfect for soft baits such as expander pellet.

For a few weeks that summer I had some great sport at Hollowell using the 17ft rod with a centrepin. The pin I use now is one I had made for me by Dave Swallow specifically for barbel, a fine reel that has proved very reliable when controlling big tench hooked under the rod top.

Eventually the weed grew and strengthened, and a more practical set-up was needed to control the fish more quickly. This consisted of a Drennan tench float rod, 8lb BS Super Shinobi main line, and 3ft of Berkley 8lb BS fluorocarbon because of the water clarity (it is wise to

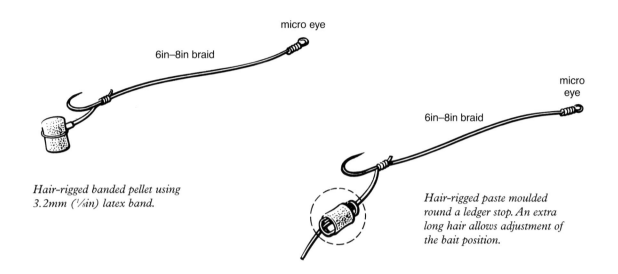

Hair-rigged banded pellet using 3.2mm (⅛in) latex band.

Hair-rigged paste moulded round a ledger stop. An extra long hair allows adjustment of the bait position.

Hollowell 10lb 8oz tench using a 17ft rod and centrepin.

93

replace this after every few fish though, because of possible knot fatigue); also 6in of iron thread 8lb BS braid made by Fenwick (though this may no longer be obtainable). I like it because it is a very dependable sinking braid: one end is tied to the hook, and the other to a stainless-steel micro eye. To facilitate a quick change when required, I carry a number of these prettied with hooks of varying size, and also hair rigs, some for use with paste and others with a band on the hair for hard

pellet use. Others are made using multi-strand of various strengths, which can, on occasion, prove more successful than braid. When fishing shallow water in bright conditions, I often camouflage this using marker pens.

One word of warning when using multi-strand: be sure to superglue all knots. I lost a big tench at Sywell one day due to a knot slipping. This tench would show itself at the west end of the dam, usually between 10am and midday, and it looked like a

Hollowell 9lb 11oz fish caught on expander pellet.

Hollowell early autumn fish taken on large pellet.

double. Many hours were spent and many traps were laid for that fish, but all in vain. It was definitely feeding, though all manner of baits from maggots to boilies were ignored. Finally, one day after feeding casters, I had a bite on a single caster with a size 18 hook buried inside it. Three seconds later, disaster. The hook was tied to multi-strand some weeks previously, but had missed being superglued and the knot slipped: one of my worst moments, and that fish wasn't seen again.

By mid-August 2001 I had taken seventy-six tench from Hollowell including other doubles of 10lb 1oz and 10lb 8oz. Few fish were under 5½lb, and most were over 6lb, and there were a satisfying number of 7lb and 8lb fish, and one at 9lb 10oz.

Over the years the old gravel patrol route across the dam had been washed away by wave movement and not been replaced. The filamentous algae was now very lush, and tench could be observed feeding in this. One would stop, hover for a

Acquaintance renewed, or a near twin?

few seconds, then tilt downwards and bury its head in the algae, staying in that position for a further few seconds; then without moving it would blow out a load of debris, keep that position for a few more seconds before slowly regaining its normal level and moving off. So any hookbait going into that mouth could be instantly rejected.

Evening sessions during previous years had not proved very rewarding. However, on one occasion I arrived at 5.30pm. A light breeze was ruffling the surface, and on approaching the previously dragged swim, I had spotted a dark shape fade into deeper water, so tench were present. The stones on the dam near the water line were rather wet and slippy, and before setting up

96

ABOVE: Paul Thompson
with a rare 4lb golden
tench he caught at White
Acres Fishery.

ABOVE: Paul Thompson
with a rare 4lb golden
tench he caught at White
Acres Fishery.

Bob Church displays a
young yellow tench
weighing exactly 8lb. This
specimen was caught at
dusk and was the 'last
fish of the day'.

Groundbait balls are catapulted to the vicinity of each end tackle.

ABOVE: *An 8lb-plus that was caught on the end of a big south-westerly wind (you can see the reeds being bent over).*

ABOVE: *An 8lb-plus January tench.*

BELOW: *Bob Church with an 8lb 2oz tench caught off the dam at Sywell in 2004.*

BELOW RIGHT: *The end of the rainbow? Weighing 10lb 7oz, maybe not. Peter just wants to catch another one a little bigger, perhaps.*

ABOVE: Keith Sanders with a strawberry-bellied beauty.

ABOVE: Dave Harman in July 1995 with 11lb 6oz of Johnson's magic.

BELOW: Chris Sullivan with an 8lb 11oz male in June 1997.

LEFT: *Wraysbury rewards. Dave Harman in June 1998 with two magnificent tench weighing 10lb 3oz and 9lb 14oz.*

BELOW: *Ferris awakens in May 2001 – Warren Hammond with his magnificent 10lb 8oz specimen.*

BELOW: *Rory Adair in May 1998, with a fine fish weighing 10lb 10oz, one of four doubles he had from Ferris that season.*

ABOVE: Keith Sanders at Sywell in 1995, with his then personal best tench weighing 10lb 4oz.

RIGHT: A decent fish from a new water is always satisfying; this was Peter's first seven from Castle Lake.

Dave Harman with his personal best tench of 11lb 8oz.

ABOVE: In June 1999 Jim Cheverall's turn came in style, with Wraysbury monsters of 10lb 3oz, 9lb 7oz and 9lb 4oz.

TOP LEFT: This beautiful, last-minute 'Wraysbury double' of 10lb 11oz was landed in June 1999.

LEFT: Keith Sanders proudly displays this fine specimen that was caught at Hollowell and weighed 10lb 13oz. Note the cyst.

In May 1998, Ferris finally delivers with the 'Blackspot', weighing 10lb 14½oz.

RIGHT: One of eight taken on pellet by Keith Sanders using centrepin.

MIDDLE RIGHT: Dave Harman with a superb brace of 11lb-plus tench in May 2001.

BELOW RIGHT: Rory Adair in June 1995 with a fine tench, heavy in spawn, weighing 12lb ½oz, the biggest ever landed at Ferris Meadows.

BELOW: Rather wet but happy. Janet Jackson with a Sywell nine-pounder, her first from the water. The sack is one of Del Romag's industrial nylon ones that he produced a few years ago with extra holes in it. Neither Peter nor Janet has ever had any trouble with them.

BELOW: Dave Harman returns the 'Black One' at Papercourt in July 2000. This lovely fish weighed 10lb 6oz.

ABOVE: Big tench seldom come better looking than this 10lb 9oz Ferris Meadow specimen.

LEFT: A very near miss on the ounces, but who cares – this was a stupendous-looking fish.

I scattered some sand, which I carry for this purpose.

Bait was expander pellet with Betaine HCI added to the water before soaking. This was before I had obtained a pellet pump, so the water used came from my garden pond rather than tap water that tench could well find less palatable.

After an hour and a half, having gone through all the usual presentations and trying without success to read some indication from the float, the breeze suddenly dropped and the surface became a flat calm. So now it was possible to overload the fine-insert crystal float with a No. 6 shot placed 2in from the hook that was set at dead depth to the algae with ¼in of float showing. This did produce a very small movement indicating that something had happened, and which wouldn't have shown in the breeze; but it was not enough to strike at.

With the surface being so calm, I picked out a 3in porcupine float many years old. With one No. 6 shot fixed 24in off the bottom, the weight of the bait settling on top of the algae sank the float to a pin head. Blows were now apparent in the swim, and with my hand on the rod butt in anticipation, I suddenly realized I wasn't breathing. Two minutes later the pin head flattened, releasing the tension, and I connected to a tench of about 7lb hooked well in the mouth, showing how far back the bait had been taken. From then on, striking at fractional lifts and dips, I landed another nine tench between 6lb and 8lb 11oz before it was too dark to see pin-head floats. All fish were hooked inside the mouth, and I had one bite off. The largest was weighed just in case it made 9lb.

Driving the few miles home in the dark, I reflected how it never ceases to amaze me that fish of that size can give such minute indications when they are feeding so confidently, and how such a subtle change in presentation decided the result. The following evening the breeze didn't drop until nearly dark. I saw one minuscule bite and netted a male of 7lb 3oz. What a difference a breeze makes!

By mid-October the tench had moved to extreme sensitive indication range. Boilies and large Solar squid and octopus pellets had been introduced during the previous two weeks, as there was an increasing problem from small roach and perch when using small baits. The last three fish fell to Solar pellets – which, incidentally, Solar stopped supplying due to lack of interest from carp anglers. This was unfortunate, because tench accepted them readily after some prebaiting.

My total catch from Hollowell that year was 116 tench. Since then the algae has not flourished on the dam, and only a handful of tench have fallen to the float.

A WINTER'S DAY 2003

The following account, entitled 'Winter Tench', was a contribution to the Tench-fishers club bulletin, written immediately after it occurred:

It's Wednesday, January 29th. A few days ago a southerly wind blew from the Sahara, but last night there was a severe frost. Today is my first opportunity to fish for two weeks, and we have north winds gusting to 50mph, a temperature of 2°C, with a wind-chill factor of minus ten. Snow flurries, and heavy snow are forecast.

Now with three score and ten years behind me I really should have more sense, but the urge to have a tench grace my net again proved stronger – especially after seeing some casters thrown into my garden pond being sampled by orfe, koi and a tench that did seem to tilt slightly to sip one in. I don't think it was wishful thinking. Also relevant was the knowledge of a short stretch of bank at Grendon which would allow me to fish with the wind at my back, and just enough calm water in front for sensitive presentation.

After filling up with diesel, and then of course having to return home to wash off the smell with coal tar soap, it was 11.30am before the umbrella was well secured. Fighting the wind to thread the 17ft rod with 3lb BS line from the centrepin took all of ten minutes. It was with great relief that I sat in the protection of the umbrella to attach a small crystal fine-insert float, and a size 18 spade hook tied to multi-strand (approximately 3lb BS) using two No. 4 shot fixed 2ft above the hook and baited with a single red maggot, and the float set at 7ft. The combined weight of hook and bait settled the float a further ¼in, so providing the wind doesn't swing too much, a lift bite should show something.

A few casters and maggots were introduced once it was determined which side of the rod tip the bait would settle if a drift were present. By this time I really was not overconfident, but at the precise moment I began to consume a cheese roll, the float indicated a movement different from that caused by the buffeting wind.

The cheese roll dropped into the maggot box instead of my lunch box, but I connected to a tench suddenly awakened from its semi-comatose condition. As I moved from the protection of the umbrella in order to play the fish away from the swim, I was once again fighting the wind as much as the fish. It was a relief to return a tench of about 6lb, and attempt to recover some feeling to my hands. I looked at the cheese roll but didn't really fancy it. Even though the maggots were also semi-comatose, some may have livened up enough to investigate, so I fed

it to a passing swan. That was a bad move, as it decided to stay with me for the rest of the session.

Remembering I had a pair of neoprene gloves with me, the sort that allows the fingers and thumb to fold back on Velcro, I put them on. This had the effect of concentrating all the intense feeling of cold to the exposed digits. Trying to control the centrepin was ridiculous.

I know for certain I am not a masochist, and the urge to land a tench in this weather had been satisfied. But just as I was counting down the final sixty seconds to packing up, I was in again with a 5lb-plus fish, the result of a reflex response to some minuscule movement of the float. The weather finally defeated me at 3.30pm after landing the last tench, about 7lb. My camera has an 11sec timer, which was barely enough time to manoeuvre my frozen body into position for the picture shown.

The reason for success was remembering a particular swim where the wind could be beaten. Nowhere else on that water would have produced on the day.

FOUR HOURS AT SYWELL

During 2004 my health problems forced on me some prolonged stays in hospital, so when Tek-Neek organized a fish-in at Sywell just before the season opened, it was doubtful I would be able to take part. Very generously I had been invited to guest fish, and while all the pegged swims were on the natural banks, I could fish from the dam.

I don't know what time fishing commenced, but after a last-minute decision, I arrived at the car park at about 8am. Loading the trolley and walking the short distance to the first swim on the dam, sometimes referred to as a 'crap' (very bad)

Grendon, 29 January 2003.

swim, I thought 'This will do'. Most tench I had taken from this spot in the past had been males, and it is unpredictable. From experience I knew roughly where the shallow water from the corner of the dam began to deepen, and where I could find 7ft depth not too far out. The only bait I had with me were some dynamite 14mm marine halibut pellets I had purchased the previous year, and before tackling up I scattered some about the swim. As it was the first time I had used these at Sywell, and I decided to start off ultra-sensitive, I did not know what the response would be.

There was very little weed showing at that time of the year, so I considered that 6lb BS line with fluorocarbon and braid of the same strength would be adequate, combined with the Drennan tench float rod and Shimano Areo GT reel. Also I was

Sywell 2004; a pre-season fish at 9lb 11oz.

MASTER TENCH FLOAT FISHER

able to use the small porcupine float necessary for the sensitivity I required. This was set a little overdepth and cocked by the bait which was hair rigged to a size 8 hook using a pellet band. The wind was south-west so I was in a fairly sheltered spot, although if it strengthened it could prove a little troublesome.

After casting, I set the float to virtually just a dot showing. Geoff, the park ranger, who had given up his Sunday to assist, was just informing me that the odd fish had been taken when the dot became fractionally larger. My response caused the rod to arch over, much to Geoff's surprise, and the first tench, a male, was duly landed.

After the second tench had been taken in the same manner, I was content, and it was time to experiment using larger floats, lying well on the bottom, and various other presentations. But whether those tench were not really partial to the pellets, or were just behaving as tench often do, I could not conjure up any obvious interest; so it was back to the original set-up, and another male was netted.

Then occurred a biteless half an hour, after which I surmised that the fish could well have moved out a little into deeper water; so raising the float, I followed, and out came tench number four.

The wind then strengthened, so I changed to the extended float method using a 2ft extension in order to sink the line beneath an increasing surface drift. This was successful in combating the drift, and also allowed me to continue using the small porcupine float, but only with more float showing as the waves were swamping a micro dot. However, the different presentation had somehow altered the overall sensitivity, because the float just disappeared and a female of 9lb 11oz was landed and photographed. By midday two more males had been taken, making a total of seven tench, which was, I believe, the biggest catch and the biggest fish of the day. Although I am sure the tench would have continued to feed all day, by this time I was ready to stop fishing, and duly made my way home, satisfied.

TO CONCLUDE

That more or less brings me up to date with my life spent tenching. I have fished Sywell a few more times, and taken a few more fish, not to halibut pellets though. I have been trying a paste made from a base mix, and flavours obtained from John Baker who specializes in barbel baits. It's early days, but flavour levels seem all important.

A trip to Grendon in late October produced eleven tench, all to expander pellets flavoured with a tiny amount of John Baker's anchovy. The terminal tackle consisted of a size 16 hook tied to multi-strand and presented 1in off the bottom. The float was once again set to a pin head. Other anglers were complaining of 'only getting taps from small stuff'. However, past experience causes me to be wary of suggesting that other anglers' interpretations might possibly be flawed. So I just remained that 'lucky so-and-so'.

My final tench of 2004, just one fish on caster, came on New Year's Eve; but four tench and a carp taken one day in early February 2005 are worth a mention. Maggots on their own accounted for perch, but only with one small shot on the bottom. Nutrabaits 'Trigga' pellet on a hair to a size 14 hook produced such tiny indications that they were unstrikable. However, pellet on the hair and two red maggots on the hook resulted in bites just positive enough to connect with, but only with no shot on the bottom. Without that precise presentation the day would probably have ended fishless.

That reminds me. After agreeing to submit this insight into my tench fishing, Bob offered me the following advice, based on his many years of successful writing. He said 'write happy'. Bearing his advice in mind I have deliberately excluded all the many fishless days I have experienced. It may still, however, be considered overlong and self-indulgent, but if it offers food for thought, then that's good. Although I doubt it will provide many answers, there are days when logic tells me alternative methods to those I am using would produce better results. However, the need for personal satisfaction overrides logic.

Earlier I stated that the only advice I could offer anyone wanting to catch bigger tench would be to fish waters where they live. At Sywell I have observed people fishing for the first time being shown how to cast a heavy bolt rig and winching in big tench; in one case a fish over 9lb. Other highly competent anglers have fished there for years and taken many fish without coming close to that weight.

The ability to catch tench consistently requires a certain level of skill. But to reiterate my opinion, the size of fish that skill produces is mostly down to luck, apart from the visual stalking and landing of an individual specimen.

Don't get me wrong, the experience of holding a big tench is a privilege, and it's no bad thing to have a goal to aim for; but I cannot correlate the size of tench to purely angling skill. However, big tench will always remain beautiful. Anglers will always derive great satisfaction involving a feel-good factor in landing a personal best – but that is all it is, personal. Even if it were a new record, the only thing it proves is that it exists.

I would suggest that as long as we can continue to enjoy catching, but also to respect this beautiful and often puzzling species of whatever size, by whatever method, without causing them any harm, let's just consider ourselves fortunate.

The most powerful driving force that feeds this sport of ours is a mixture of anticipation and optimism. But if you also harbour a desire for a personal best tench, well you never know, Lady Luck might just decide to sit by your side during your next tench session.

4 Fifty-Five Years Hunting Big Tench

by Peter Jackson

The first tench I caught was more than fifty years ago, and I just cannot believe that it is so long ago that I put the first ones on the bank. I used to catch them from the River Lea, local to my home. Methods were simple, just what was used generally on the river at the time. A piece of peacock quill for a float, and one or two shot to hold the bait on the bottom – and that was it, simplicity. There was no talk of *rigs* – they were confined to sailing ships. When I fished the weir pools I mostly used the ledger, and again, it was very simple, just a coffin lead stopped about 9in from the hook.

The approach was not that of the dedicated catcher of big fish, but you just fished for whatever was in front of you at the time. I was, after all, only about twelve years old and just wanted to catch fish, any fish: if tench were present I fished for them; gudgeon, and I fished for them. I didn't care, fish were fish, and I fished for whatever was there at the time.

Most life-long anglers have, at some time in their early angling career, a defining moment, an episode that takes a hold of one's life forever more, and sets us on a particular course that, with few variations, is for life. For me it happened one wet evening on Dobb's Weir. I had been night fishing for some time, probably two or three years at least, and just loved the atmosphere, the enfolding velvety darkness that added to the whole mystery of it all. I

was fishing for bream, as most of us did then, and the weir pool held quite a lot of them; they were not very big, about 4lb or so was the sort of size we expected to catch. The usual approach was to chuck in a great load of stodge: bran, layers' mash and stale bread was what I used. It was heaved in, usually in the late afternoon, to give the bream a chance to get their heads down in the evening. That was the thinking behind it.

Thus it was that particular night. I sat on the gravel watching a lump of bread paste swinging in the breeze, hanging just off the rod tip. The rod, as a matter of interest, was a seven-footer, built cane with a wonderful set in the tip, the sort of thing that was in vogue at the time for all sorts of fishing that did not involve floats. The business end was a coffin lead of about an ounce, stopped by a BB shot about 9in from a size 8 of indeterminate make and bend, though it was eyed. The hook was held on to the line with the usual bundle of grannies. Illumination of the bobbin was by a candle in a tin, the sort that contained about a gallon of creosote; the top of the can was cone-shaped with a wide top, about 2in or so in diameter. With a door cut in the side and bent open, it made a very serviceable and windproof candle light, and the cone-shaped top made an excellent chimney.

That was how I was fishing on this particular night. I had no thoughts of tench, though they were occasionally caught in the weir pool, mostly in the slacker areas by the diving board, not in the stream area I was fishing. Despite the rain I was enjoying myself; I had caught a couple of bream that had battled in the usual fashion, going stiff and violently rolling their eyes. Tackle-testing stuff!

Then the bobbin shot up and I struck into a solid resistance that really pulled. The pull was such that rod and line felt threatened, something I had not experienced before, except when hooking the odd pike when perch fishing. Wanless spinning rods were not meant for pulling substantial fish out of weir pools, and my little rod bent much more than Alexander ever intended it to. After much lug and tug, I beached the, by then, totally exhausted fish, and it lay, golden-flanked, on the gravelly shallows. Never had I seen such a big fish: whatever did it weigh? I had no idea, nor had I any way of finding out. But yes, the pub, of course, the Fish and Eels, they could weigh it for me. Off to the pub I went, the fish wrapped in the wet pillowcase that I had brought my groundbait in.

When a rather small schoolboy entered a pub at that time he was usually asked to leave. However, if he is dripping wet and is clutching an equally wet white bag, that of its own volition twitches and moves, that does cause a lull. Before anyone could turn me out, I told the man behind the bar what I wanted: 'Please, I have caught a big fish, and I would really like to know how much it weighs!' I babbled. There was a pregnant pause while he thought about it, then the bag was scooped from the bar. 'I'll see what I can do,' he said. Conversation in the bar returned to normal as he went off on his surprise errand. I waited.

'Well, it's 4lb 14oz,' he said when he returned. 'In the bag, surely,' I mumbled. 'No, just the fish. I was most careful about that, weighed it on my wife's kitchen scales, I did,' he said, as he passed the bag with the fish in back to me over the bar.

Staggered, I just gaped at him, but eventually managed to thank him, and turned to leave. The noise of voices in the bar rose considerably. 'What was the bait?' 'Was it strong line?' 'Was it from far out?' There was a barrage of questions that I barely managed to field before I fled back into the rain. I got back to my gear, all soaked. The rats had finished most of my bait but I did not care. I laid the bag in the shallows and gently eased the fish out into the golden glow of the candle. Truly I thought it beautiful, the golden scales intensified in the yellow candle light. Slowly righting itself, it gently swum off into the darkness. I was sad to see it go, yet glad that it had come to no harm after a trip to the pub with a schoolboy. Neither fish nor schoolboy could have had such an experience before.

TACKLE AND TACKLE MAKING

That fish lit a fire that has never been extinguished; for various reasons it may have diminished to a glow, only to burst forth again when a new challenge came along. The late fifties, early sixties were a very different period for fishing to what we have now, and really it is more about the mental attitude that prevailed at the time. There was not that much in the way of tackle to be had, and most of the books in print were so antiquated that they had virtually no value to anyone in search of knowledge. At that time anglers had to make a great deal of their tackle bits, which in itself could be a real challenge. Rod building was well covered – though not as now, when you buy a set of blanks and fit pre-formed grips, whip on a few rings and go fishing. In those days it was the real thing, from buying raw Tonkin poles, how to harden the skin with a blowlamp (I later did this for real at Chapman's, the rod builders in Ware, along with many of the other tasks associated with making split cane). There were also instructions on how to make the wooden formers that were used in planing up the tapered sixty-degree sections that made up the hexagonal shape of the finished section.

Every aspect of tackle making was covered in those books. Gluing and binding was a bit of a dark art involving mostly animal glue, which dissolved in water; that was why there was so much emphasis on good marine varnish, a copal varnish made from resins of tropical trees imported from our then still mighty Empire. Rings were terrible really, made either of steel wire and chrome-plated, or with harder-wearing centres made of agate, if you were well off. Other centres that were around were 'agatine', a much more fragile substitute; or porcelain, heavy and seriously fragile. I used to carry spare ones along with ghastly sticky cloth tape that stuck to everything when you tried to use it. About an hour after taping on the ring it would start to unravel, and then fall off, so the whole process had to be carried out again.

Some things could be bought, though, leads and shot and such items. Spinners, spoons and plugs were often home-made, and anglers whose formative years touched on the fifties and sixties certainly did not regard making them as odd. There was certainly a good deal of pleasure in the making of some items, though I did baulk at the making of built cane from scratch.

Drop Me a Line and *Stillwater Angling* did not initially seem to make that much impact on me, though Richard Walker's catching of the then record carp certainly did, and that, along with Hitchin Club winning the *Daily Mirror* competition, lit a fire that has burned brightly ever since; together they were the catalyst that produced the reality of catching fish by design, and I was swept up by it all from quite an early age – all I wanted was to catch big fish. Tench in particular were what I wanted; I had already caught one, and so had experienced the thrill of catching a nationally notable fish. Carp were out of reach: from what I read I knew that I had not, at that time, got the near-unattainable qualities that one needed to fish for carp; perhaps one day I may work up to such heights, but I did not really find them as attractive as red-eyed tench.

For two or three years I fished Hatfield Forest, pleasant fishing, where I learned a few new methods and refined some others. Although it was fun, the fishing was not really of exceptional quality, and in the time I spent there I only had two four-pounders, the best of them 4lb 6oz. I was far too late, the fishing having peaked several years previously; the late Alan Vare had caught 5lb-plus fish there. However, there was a first opportunity to fish from a boat for tench, which was enjoyable and different. For the first time I was able to use a new float rod that I had bought myself, an Apollo Taperflash, the 10ft 6in version, and it was all that was claimed of them, light and with a crisp action. The noise they made, though, was never mentioned in their advertising. Whenever a fish was played, it was like a muted musical saw, and the harder the fish pulled, the higher the note it played. Athough I never had any trouble with mine, they were prone to internal rust in the steel tip section; also the lower sections were quite fragile, being very thin-walled aluminium tube. A dent was disastrous, and often meant the affected section would need to be replaced. But despite its potential for disaster, I used the rod for several years without fault, and I eventually sold it for what I paid for it. The only musical fishing rod I have ever had!

As time went on and I became more adventurous, I tried other places than my local stretches of the Lee. The gravel pits around Nazeing were all tried, though only one produced tench, the pit behind Carthagena lock – and I think I only caught about two, and those were each only a couple of pounds. It was evidently a different story in the mid-eighties when Bob fished there.

Angling Times and later *Fishing* magazine gave me just what I needed at that time: information, always the essential nourishment of big fish angling. At that time the diet was very spartan indeed, consisting mainly of tiny news items that these days look like advertisements in *The Times* personal column. Publications, such as they were, were far more conservative than they are now. This, then, was the sort of background that I was using to gain my information.

The breakthrough was 'a lake in Bedfordshire' that popped up regularly in *Angling Times*. I forget who it was that 'let it out of the bag' by calling it Whitbreads; I suspect it was Frank Guttfield. Whomsoever it was, it gave me just the hint that I needed, and the lake was soon located. The final bit of information was obtained from *Guide to Angling Waters, South East England*, a Bernard Venables' book. Southill Park, for that was where it was, rated as paradise found!

The very first time I went there the lake was shrouded in quite a thick fog, and you could see little further than the rod end. My travelling companion, Cyril, and I had no idea of what the lake looked like, apart from a picture feature that Frank Guttfield had done for *Angling* magazine some time before, though it did not give an overall picture of the water. We walked along the road that ran around the lake until we seemed well away from everybody, and set up to fish.

Our approach was the same as the one we had used on other waters: 4lb breaking strain, $\frac{1}{4}$oz bomb, stopped about a foot from a size 6 Mustad 496, a hook we had previously used for chub fishing with some success. On the hook was impaled a big lump of flake that was cast about 15yd or so. A couple of balls of leaden groundbait followed. But nothing happened, not at all, not a bite.

By early afternoon the fog had started to clear, and we could see a little more of the water, and also the source of the rhythmic swishing that had been going on. Ever since we had started fishing there it had been going on: plop, shortly followed by swish; I had to find out what it was, so I went to have a look.

I had never seen the like of it, except in pictures: two Mark IVs set up on rests so they were nicely aligned and parallel, at a height at the butt that put them in easy reach of the angler sat by them. As I gaped at this, the man struck at thin air. Not a sign of a bite had I seen, and at the time I thought he was slashing at little roach. He did have a net out, but I could not see what was in its dark depths. I went back to my static rods.

Towards dusk he started to pack up, and I just had to know what was in that keepnet. I could not believe the contents: two lovely big females and a male that was a little smaller; about 5$\frac{1}{4}$lb each for the females, and the male a little smaller, at about 4lb or so. I had to catch some of these wonderful fish for myself.

After a good many false starts on future visits, I did manage to get a few fish, though they were mostly small, certainly smaller that the ones I had seen at first. Though I was catching a few fish, the problems were mounting up. Fishing at range was not a scene that many people had addressed, so at that time there were no ready-made solutions.

Hooks

One thing that exercised my mind quite a lot was that of ledger stops. We all used split shot at that time, and what I eventually did was this: I used a simple clove hitch holding a piece of valve rubber, which was fronted by a BB shot. The result was a stop that was immovable and fairly durable. I also graduated to a split-cane carp rod. Everything else was destroyed at the wheel that was Southill. It was totally the rod to have, an icon of the time, and it was truly a quite good rod to use, with a sweet forgiving action and power enough to put an ounce of lead a hundred yards away from you if needed. Even with bulky bait such as a biggish piece of flake, seventy yards was possible. Of course, one needed good sharp hooks at that sort of range, and the sharpening stone was always in use. The hooks of the time needed constant attention, and it was not unusual to discard half a dozen in a session. Either the points were blunted or bent over, or the whole hook opened out.

It seems very strange now, in an age of chemically sharpened hooks and much improved materials and designs, but I sharpened all my hooks and tested each one before it was tied on. For sharpening I tried all manner of stones and abrasives, as did most of the other people I fished with, and in the end settled for an Arkansas stone, a natural material that cut beautifully. I understand that it does in fact originate from that area of the United States.

It took a little while to get the point right; at first my efforts would just cause the hook to plough along the skin in the inside of the mouth, only taking hold in the edge of the fish's lip but making a bit of a mess on the way there, which was not to be tolerated. But eventually I got it right, and fish were hooked properly wherever the hook first touched. In tandem with that I started to seriously use de-barbed hooks to see if it made that much difference to the number of fish that fell off, or whether it made any difference at all.

The first thing to be noticed was that once hooked, they stayed on as before – even on a totally slack line the fish stayed on. Gradually I convinced myself that for what I was doing, crushing the barb down, really flattening it, was worth doing. Probably the best effect of this was the ease of removing the hook when the fish was landed. Damage was really minimal, the tiniest of puncture marks, very important if in the course of a season that fish is going to visit the bank a few times.

When using worms, I did revert to barbed hooks, only much later using a sliver of rubber on a barbless hook to keep the bait on – and yes, it does work. Later still I used those little rubber line stops, much used when fishing with sliding floats. I have ever since used barbless hooks for nearly all of my fishing and I have a huge selection to choose from, no longer having to doctor barbed designs. Currently Peter Drennan's most excellent Starpoint design is my hook of choice, even in quite small sizes.

Lines

When one looks at lines that are available now, and what we had then, we are spoilt for choice. Just one catalogue that I have lists thirty-six different ones, each in a range of breaking strains (this includes a number of braids, of course). When I fished at Southill we had a realistic choice of perhaps six. Most of those were terrible; the least awful of them was Platil, and I used it for some time – though in truth, it was not very good. To give some idea of just how bad some of these lines were, I had bought some 'Sportex Perlyl', a green line that was visually quite appealing. I had that in a breaking strain of about 5lb or so. What I did to test it was to run out about seventy yards of it, tie one end to a tree, and see how far I had to go to break it. I did that test three times, and each time I went ten yards before it broke. It was like the knicker elastic that one dreamed about. I didn't use it.

Despite the odds, we all caught fish. I managed most times to catch my share, but Bill Quinlan caught just about everybody else's, too! The more I fished with him, the more I realized that he was rather special as an angler, and as a person, too.

BAITS AND BAITING

Sausage rusk was something that Bill and John Simpson put me on to, the *raison d'être* of this stuff being to bind and bulk out the humble banger. It has been around for a very long time, certainly seventy years or more, and for most of that time anglers have used it for groundbait. What Bill and John did was to utilize the link ledger to carry groundbait: when mixed properly – that is, just damped down, enough for it to bind together when squeezed hard – it was quite easy to mould around the shot and cast it out; when it hit the water the ball of bait burst, leaving very little on the shot, but making a column of rusk particles from the surface to the bottom. The really good part of keeping the mix as dry as possible was that individual particles would rise up from the bottom as the larger lumps disintegrated. John demonstrated that to me in the margins, recreating experiments that he had carried out originally in the swimming pool at Eton College! ('At night,' he said!). There is still some mileage in both the method, and also sausage rusk as a groundbait.

A small contribution that I made was to use rusk as a hookbait. Taking a handful of groundbait I added more water, and after kneading, it was possible to create a nice smooth paste. Such a mix would last about an hour or so before totally disintegrating into a little cone of rusk particles.

Even the keenest of specimen hunters will doze in the soporific warmth of a summer morning, as I did on one particular occasion. But the cry of 'You gorra bite!' dragged me into wakefulness. Can't be, I thought, as I swung the rod up. But a fish was on, on a piece of paste that had long before dissolved into a little pile of rusk. The fish had just sucked it up, hook and all. After that, many more fish were taken in like manner, but deliberately.

A little variation that worked really well was tipping the hook with a tiny crust cube. It looked ridiculous: I was using either a size 6 or 4 at the time for paste fishing. Nevertheless, not much more than a crumb was set on the bend, then the whole lot was covered with a lump of paste. Why it worked I don't know, but it did. Bites increased quite a lot by doing this, and some days it seemed to be the edge that saved a blank.

Another bait that caught a few fish were swan mussels, easily gathered in the margins. And what swan mussels they were! Absolutely enormous – some that I gathered from the area near the boat-house had shells 10in long. One could easily get four hookbaits from one of these. Why they were so big I don't know, but the biggest I found would span a tea plate.

Casting out these big lumps of groundbait took a heavy toll on rods, and before long my carp rod took on a hefty set. The set did not affect its performance, but the sag just had to be seen. Eventually the inevitable happened, and I took home a bundle of splintered cane.

RODS, KNOTS AND BIVVIES

At that time, a new wonder material was just coming on the scene: fibreglass. This amazingly light material took the angling world by storm, and soon a good number of people were sporting sunshine-yellow fishing rods. Most of them were home-made, because we were still in the realm of home-built fishing tackle.

The first ones I made for fishing at Southill were at the unheard-of length of 11ft 3in. The most radical thing about them was that the handles were two separate pieces of cork, rather than one continuous piece. This idea I soon dropped, because in the rain it was an absolute nightmare, always sliding away from one's forearm either into the armpit, or worse, sliding up the outside of the arm. I felt, and still do, that the old rod makers had it right, that a continuous handle was more suitable for all-round use.

I was buying all my gear from the well-known north London shop, Don's of Edmonton, where as well as tackle of all sorts, there was a constant stream of advice and tips. Of particular value was a good reliable knot for spade-end hooks. This was

At this time we made just about everything. These sorts of books were bread and butter to us – just look at the alarm.

devised by the late Alan Vare, and was a great improvement on the Domhof knot in general use at the time. I and several others had found that the Domhof could be unreliable, whereas Alan's knot, when tied properly, was just the opposite: I have never found it wanting, and nor has anybody else that has used it. We could not fish without good knots; anything else we could get by on. A real advantage of this knot is that when it is pulled tight, the reel line is drawn into the middle of the knot where it is held by a crossover. This is worth practising because it is very secure, and there is very little, if any, loss of strength. For exhaustive details of this knot, see Freshwater Fishing by Falkus and Buller, published by Macdonald and Janes.

After two or three seasons I was stopping over for two or three days at a time; nowadays this is no big discomfort, but back then, nobody had invented bivvies, and there were no lightweight materials to make them out of. All that was available was cotton canvas, which was really heavy, especially when wet. Even obtaining such material was near impossible, so any shelter was an improvised affair, usually plastic sheeting and garden canes; even bits of tarpaulin were pressed into service. I managed to get hold of a small canvas tent – and I mean *really* small, so that when I stretched out, either my head stuck out of the front or my feet stuck out of the back; if I wanted to stay dry, the only way I could sleep was with my

The little tent at Southill before the flood.

knees drawn up. But even that was envied by some!

One weekend we had a storm with really heavy rain, but I sat out fishing, smugly thinking that I would be all right, all my gear would be nice and dry in the tent. But the verge where I was pitched sloped gently downhill; my little tent was pitched halfway down, and the rain was heavy enough to partially flood the road and turn it into a temporary river. And the river ran right through my little tent, in at the front and out of the back, carrying all before it. As luck would have it I had recently become the proud owner of a camp bed, so at least my bedding stayed dry. Everything else was seized by the joyous flood and bowled down the road: the saucepan, tins of beans, sausages, all manner of camping detritus. What a mess! It took ages to dry it all out and pick the twigs out of the sausages. After that I pitched in the front garden of an empty cottage just up the road. There, the only problem was the deer pinging the guy cords in the middle of the night with their antlers – very disturbing the first time it happened. By staying overnight there were a number of advantages, not least that dawn was very early, at least an hour, or even more, than it was for most others – except Bill Quinlan, of course.

Fishing so early posed some problems that I had not previously encountered. Generally in the Lee valley, even in those days, there was a great deal of light pollution. Southill was not affected by such things, and darkness was complete and Stygian; even quite large bits of silver paper were very hard to see. In the end I used two bits of peacock quill crossed over the line and laid flat on the ground; I often lay on the ground with my nose but a few inches from them in my efforts to see them in the intense, velvety dark. Frequently I was hit in the face as the quills flew, and there followed an undignified scramble as I tried to get to the rod and deal with the fish on the other end. If ever there were people awaiting an invention, it was us awaiting the arrival of the Betalight.

None of us had caught or even seen a 6lb fish, though there were rumours. Just about every water I have ever fished has apocryphal tales of fish that are much bigger than any that anyone has personal experience of, and Southill was no different; indeed, there was a rumour of a seven-pounder, no less. That fish was apparently caught by the mysterious Spencer, but nobody could put a face to the name. The spot where the fish was caught was, of course, known as Spencer's Hole.

Most weekends Alan Brown would come to the lake, on either Saturday evenings or Sunday mornings. At that time he worked in a shoe shop, so his weekends were restricted by the shop hours. One particular Sunday morning he arrived, all out of breath as usual, and as there was nowhere else available that he fancied, he put his rod rests a few yards up the bank from me in Spencer's Hole. Once he was comfortably ensconced, he started sorting out his bait and groundbait. And what a nightmare that was: scalded maggots in sausage rusk. The trouble was, he had put live maggots in the dry rusk, and then tipped boiling water on the lot, so the result was more suited to bricklaying than fishing.

'Well, it's all I have, so in it goes,' he said. I am sure there was little hope or enthusiasm that morning as he sat behind his pair of Avocets. Interestingly his rods, self-built, were markedly different to everyone else's in one respect, and that was, the rings were whipped on using 4lb breaking-strain monofil that, when varnished, gave the whippings a not unpleasant translucent finish that was much admired.

That morning I am sure he did not expect to do much more than admire them himself. The tennis-ball-size lumps of

Alan Brown with his 6lb 6oz fish. It came third in the notable fish competition that was run by Fishing *magazine at the time (1966).*

groundbait sank like stones, giving every impression of retaining their shape for at least a fortnight, and they did not inspire confidence. He sat back in the sun with a cup of coffee and a cigar. After about an hour or so the dough bobbin sailed up and a most surprised Alan swept up the Avocet, which took on a very satisfying curve. The dispute went on for some time, and the longer it went on, the more interested we all became. Eventually the fish was drawn over the net and lifted out.

Laid on the grass it was obvious that it was rather special, and a number of us gathered round for the 'ooh and aah thasabigun' ritual. A carrier bag was produced, and the fish slid into it, then all was suspended under an 8lb Salter balance.

After due deliberation it was decided that it weighed 6lb 6oz, after subtraction of the weight of the bag. What a whacker!

SUMMERS AT SOUTHILL

In all, I had about seven summers at lovely Southill, and in all that time I saw only one other fish over the magic number. It went to the rod of a friend of many years and fellow member of the Herts-Chiltern anglers, Bob Carter. That fish was 6lb 1oz.

Southill was a windy water, the wind nearly always blowing in one's face, which caused all sorts of problems at times. In hindsight, most of the problems were those of our own making. Particulate ground-bait and maggots would naturally cause tiny bites as the fish inched their way along feeding on tiny items. Dealing with these brought about all sorts of strange

Ernie Wakelin, for many years the bailiff at Southill Lake. He lived in a tiny cottage about a hundred yards from the lake. The cottage had no services at all, and he lived like a hermit of old. He used to send us Christmas cards made of wallpaper.

solutions, including sinking most of the rod under the waves, putting the tip about two feet down.

Bill Quinlan's way suited me better and I used it a lot, though it was rather hypnotic. This was to fish with his rods (we were using two) so the tips were about two feet above the waves. Dough bobbins were used, positioned about eighteen inches beyond the rod tip – very small bobbins, about the diameter of a pencil end and certainly not much larger, or the constant movement would unsettle and move the small weights in use at the time. As the depth at the dam wall was about three feet or so, we had to use a little ingenuity to put on a dough bobbin. After casting, the line was sunk in the normal manner. Once it was settled, the pick-up was opened and the rod swung back over the shoulder until horizontal. In that position it was easy to catch the line and put on a tiny bobbin; then when the rod was back in the correct position, the resultant slack could be taken up. Reaching forward and winding gently through the bobbin, one could get the amount of overhang required without even getting out of the chair. Tench, being contrary, would often try to pick up the first bait when one is dealing with the second, and it did give a chance to have a go at them when they tried it on.

Fishing like this in a big wind required a lot of concentration, as the lines would tend to stick in the waves. That would cause the line to slip from wave crest to wave crest, making the bobbins dance rhythmically up and down. Set right, and they would be synchronous, rising and falling together. A bite usually showed by a slight pause in the steady rise and fall.

However, there was an unforeseen hazard in fishing like this, because left undisturbed to hang in the breeze for long periods, dough bobbins can bake on to the line like a brick. Once or twice I did lose fish because the bobbin was immovable, toasted by the sun and wind; it was only much later that the problem was solved satisfactorily.

WE JOIN THE TENCH FISHERS

During the time that I fished at Southill I applied to join the Tenchfishers, a national group that had raised the profile of the species. The application was successful and I duly joined. It was only much later that I found out that there had been some discussion over my joining, because it seemed that the tench I had caught at that time were in dispute! I had, at the time, caught fifteen fish of 5lb or more, a figure that was little short of miraculous, they thought. There were not that many who had caught more than one or two of such a weight in the group. My then regular fishing companion, and, it has to be said, transport, also joined – Michael (Ginger) Davis; together we made the long trip to Leicester for what was to be a momentous meeting for us. We met with real angling luminaries such as Terry Coulson and John Ellis, both of whom were prominent on the scene at the time. For me though, far more important was meeting two Suffolk men, one a sign writer, the other at that time a welder. The van they arrived in had on its sides the logo L.A.H. It turned out that his name was Len Head and his welding brother was Ted. We remained friends until his untimely death a few years ago. I miss him still.

At the meeting we went through the mysteries of the reporting scheme and how Dr Terry envisaged its workings, with lots of charts and diagrams in different colours. I was baffled. I did join, though, and we both committed ourselves to form filling. The plus side of joining was the rotary

Entitlement to fish at Sywell, early seventies style.

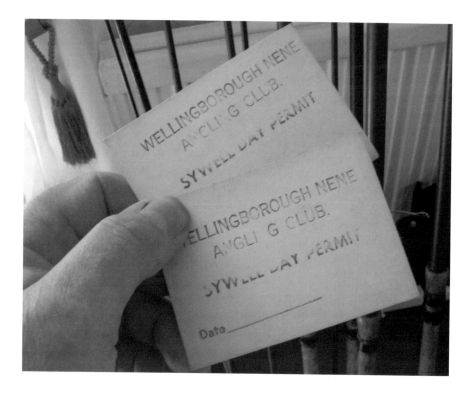

letter, a sort of postal discussion group that was ongoing. The letter circulated around the members who added articles and comment as it visited each member. At that time there were only about fifteen members so it was not too cumbersome to operate. Anglers generally were not so keen to join an outfit that had no water of its own and had no intention of pursuing such a thing.

I think that at the time such an exchange of ideas was a revelatory experience for us all. The whole specimen group thing had only just begun to flower, and there were still many voices raised that said that the idea could not work – that for the mass of anglers, catching big fish by design was just dreamland. We were young and optimistic and we believed in ourselves. We were following the edicts of the Lord of Hitchin.

I fished for several seasons at Southill, but no big ones came my way, though I did get quite a number of five-pounders. Fishing there for me came to a close when control of the water went to a syndicate. A fitting finale for me was that I had a 5lb 14oz, equalling my previous best; this was my last fish from the water.

FISHING AT SYWELL

The following close season Ginger and I decided to try a water that Bob Carter had put me on to: Sywell. To be honest, I was not that keen on the idea of fishing a reservoir, and envisaged something like those of the lower Lea valley: Walthamstow, the William Girling and suchlike water. How wrong I was.

Access to the water was via the Wellingborough and Nene Angling Club. Joining was done through local tackle shops, who also supplied day tickets for the reservoir.

Bob Church plays an 8lb tench from (2004) Sywell at sunset.

There was no charge for these tickets, one just asked for them.

Those who go there now would not believe how different it was then. At that time the place was run by Higham Ferrers and Rushden Water Company; it was strictly private, with no access to the general public – only us anglers were allowed in. We soon found that the rule was strictly enforced by the engineer who lived on the estate. The first visit we made, we were greeted by the said engineer at the gate, shotgun under arm. 'What do you want?' he said. 'We want to go fishing, sir,' we said. Shotguns induce respect. Having shown our tickets, we were graciously shown in and told where to park, just a short track to the car park. Much later, he would tell all that would listen that those Jacksons spent their honeymoon there, fishing the water and sleeping in a lay-by on the A45.

Anybody who sees the place for the first time cannot fail to be struck by the beauty of the water. When we saw it there were no joggers, dog walkers, screaming kids,

Evening at Sywell from the oak tree – just sublime.

picnickers, none of the accoutrements of the 'country park'. Do we create country parks for people who have no conception of countryside and how to behave there?

Our first day's fishing there was not very successful, as neither of us had even a bite. Nevertheless, I can think of few nicer places to have a blank. We fished at the cow-shed swim, which gave a reasonable view of quite a lot of the water, especially the left-hand arm. There was also considerable activity towards the top of the arm, though it was too far away to know what was going on. On the second day I decided to take a walk up there to see what it was all about, and when I got there I found a

Bob Church at Sywell, cranking in another one.

small group of people fishing in a couple of double swims. One pair was husband and wife, the other I later found to be Ron Kyte, a charming and slightly eccentric school teacher. The couple, I was surprised to find, were none other than Mr and Mrs Church.

We fell to talking, and Bob suggested that I moved into the area where he was fishing after he left. That I did, and during the following few days, while Bob and Beryl were working, I started to catch some fish using the methods they had been using. A visit to Smith's paper shop and tackle emporium, and we were armed to the teeth with a big heap of open-ended swim-feeders and a gallon of maggots. On the way back to the water we stopped off at Bob's house to tell him how it was going. After a brief chat we left to go back to the water, Bob's final words ringing in our ears. 'You will get a six in the next few days,' he said. What rubbish, I thought. The next day I was back at his front door to tell

A milestone for me, the first six-pounder I had caught.

118

What can one say of this drag, apart from WOW!

him I had cracked it, and that a six-pounder had slid into the net. Swim-feeder and maggot was the magic, so thanks, Bob.

Swim Dragging

That was the beginning of a golden period for us on the water, and a lot of new methods evolved there. Swim dragging in particular was something that we really got to grips with, and using a boat added a new dimension; we were able to do a proper job on a swim that could easily be sixty yards long. One year the weed was so bad that I decided I would really sort it out, and so made a rather larger than usual drag. At a little over eight feet wide, it was a drag to be reckoned with, including a 2,000lb breaking strain rope: all in all a monster. We loaded it on the punt (yes, we had boats available in those days, so why not now, I wonder?) and took it down the west arm and assembled it there. Put together it looked, hmm, intimidating. After some discussion with my helpers – there were about eight of us – we sketched out a plan of action. The drag was taken out to the end of the swim and with a combination of a pull on the rope and a push from the punt, the drag was on its way. Great eruptions of bubbles marked its path along the floor of the reservoir. Peter Wheat loved it: 'I've never seen anything like it, a giant hedge-hog, a bloody great hedgehog!' he said; and that was what it became known as, the hedgehog.

119

We cleared three swims with it, right out in the centre of the arm. It would be nice to say that it was a resounding success and that we caught lots of fish, but it was not to be. The weather changed catastrophically, and plunging temperatures and icy rain saw to it that very little was caught. Looking back on it, my feeling about it is that, given fair and settled conditions, the outcome could have been very different. We did, after all, catch more than elsewhere on the reservoir, and it did clear swims that stayed that way for more than two seasons, which was an unexpected bonus.

More modest swims were still dealt with using a hand drag just thrown from the bank. Even that though, with a bit of effort, would create an area forty yards by ten that was just about weed free.

As ever when fishing is that good, the word got around, the number of people fishing started to creep up, and we were joined by others from all over the country. The down side to that was that a significant amount would not clear their own swims, preferring to make use of the hard work of others. In turn, that gave rise to devious ploys to protect our own hard work. One of the best I saw was by fellow contributor, Keith Sanders. He and a friend would bait areas beyond the substantial reed margin that at that time went round most of the water. No effort was made to clear the reeds prior to fishing, this making his baited area not only inaccessible but also hidden. The following morning, Keith turned up to fish his baited swim. What a sight he and his mate presented, both laden with tackle, and on the head of each, an upturned kitchen table. These they planted out in the reeds, a comfortable fishing platform whenever they wanted it: what can one say of that – just brilliant!

Our own methods were rather more prosaic compared with Keith: using a rush knife, a section of reed was cut out, and when we wished to fish, we just parked it to one side and anchored it. When the session was over the rushes were just floated back into the hole and anchored with a couple of sticks. The weed that was dragged out was put in spots that had not been cleared, all to keep the pressure off the going swims and to confuse the enemy.

Sywell at that time was different to anywhere else, and I guess that nowadays there are very few waters like it. It was rather like an exclusive club, and we did more or less as we pleased, though we never abused the trust implicit in being able to fish there. The sort of thing I mean was that after a morning's fishing, the majority just wound in, stuck the hook in the butt ring, and went off for lunch, leaving the tackle where it was on the bank. If the weather was at all inclement, then everything was left under a pole-less brolly. Lunchtime was a vista of brollies flat to the ground, green puddings all around the banks, and not a soul in sight, nor likely to be until the evening when all returned to fish.

The end tackles that we used were simplicity itself, just an open-ended feeder on a short link; the hook-length was also kept short, about 4–6in. Hook size, depending on the way the day progressed, was anything from a size 6 to a 16. The feeders I used were of clear plastic, rather than the green ones that seem to have practically universal favour. The clear plastic ones are all but invisible in water. The other reason I like open-ended feeders is that the hook can be buried inside the feeder for casting.

Though I had caught six-pounders in the first season there, the fishing was not that much better than Southill, a difference of ounces only and so no large change in the size of fish caught; the average, however, was higher. This was mostly because the 1lb to 3lb fish evident in catches at

Southill did not occur at Sywell, which meant that we caught quite a lot more 5lb fish than previously. Then, as now, it is the remarkable average size that makes Sywell a unique place to fish.

IN SEARCH OF THE BIG ONE

In the early seventies I had a great hunger for big fish. Janet and I had found a lake in north Norfolk during the close season that looked nice and seemed to have some big fish in it, and so we decided to have a few days there in the early season. The water did, apparently, have some previous form in the shape of 7lb-plus fish, and because I had not, at that time, caught one – or, for that matter, even seen one on the bank – off we went to Norfolk.

When we arrived we had a bit of a surprise. First of all there was a bivvie on the bank: that on its own was remarkable, and much more so were its inhabitants, none other than Kevin Clifford and his wife. Why were they there? I wondered; but after a bit of a chat it turned out that what we had found was none other than the water known at the time as 'The Marsh', that had produced in the past large numbers of six-pounders to the Broadland Specimen Group. Full of hope we set up near the old boat house, fully expecting to stack them up. We did not, however, and in the three days that we were there, only one fish was caught. That fell to Kevin, an ounce or two over 7lb – and that was it, no other fish caught by anybody, a 250-mile round trip for nothing. All we got were some rather nice pictures of the estate, and a brolly that was kicked to death by an ill-tempered horse. 'The Marsh' simply faded from the scene, and the fish, as far as I know, just died out – which is rather sad, really.

Kevin Clifford with a 7lb 8oz tench from the 'Marsh', north Norfolk. I failed miserably there.

On the way home we decided that it might be a good idea to go to the Southern Leisure Centre because one of the lakes, Vinnetrow, had produced a seven-pounder a couple of weeks before, so we would try there. That extended our round trip to nearly 500 miles. Not much for a first 'seven' is it? Just to make it interesting the journey was through central London, and the rest of it on 'A' roads, with no bypasses, motorway or any of that modern stuff – a hell of a journey.

At that time we had had an Escort van fitted out for long-stay fishing, with a spring interior mattress and a two-burner stove with grill; rods were stored in the roof in lengths of plastic drainpipe. All in all it was a cramped but very friendly arrangement; the only down side was that in winter, one's head froze to the back door!

A few weeks earlier, and that fish would have been over the magic 7lb. Here, 6lb 13oz from the Southern Leisure Centre, Vinnetrow lake – hat courtesy of Bob Church!

The Southern Leisure complex was quite interesting, dug during the war for raw materials for Mulberry harbour, part of the D-Day invasion plan. Some of the lakes were not very deep; Vinnetrow, for instance, was only about eight feet or so, just a nice depth for either float or lead. There was no need to fish very far out, as the fish seemed to mainly patrol the margins. That was the way we opted to fish it,

only about twenty yards or so and a sort of Sywell attack, maggots and groundbait in a double swim, just for a change. Janet and I usually fished well apart, but on that occasion we didn't. For the first couple of days there was little to show for our efforts, just fish of 4lb or so. The local gypsies tried to buy the van, but they didn't seem to understand that without it we could not get back home – strange people.

The third morning started quietly enough, with yet another four for me, but nothing for Janet. I went off for a short break, and when I got back she was like the Cheshire cat. I didn't really have to ask, but I did anyway, knowing what I was about to be told: 'It's the big one, on your rod too, what a result!' she squeaked, hardly able to contain herself. I looked, and sure enough, it was a fish that a few weeks previously had weighed well over 7lb. We weighed it, and just could not believe what we saw: 6lb 13oz, there was no justice. Though it was, at the time, the biggest that either of us had caught, I think we both felt a little cheated. What a difference a couple or three ounces make.

NEW TECHNOLOGY

In the early to mid-seventies, a lot of things were starting to come together. NASA was at that time a real and positive force, and new technology in rods, reels and of course the Optonic was being pulled together to really change the shape of fishing, probably for ever. And the final refinement that was to enable anglers to fish for extended periods: the bivvie was born. There had, of course, been odd shelters tried, but none were very successful. Most often one would see people crouched under a brolly that had a polythene sheet skirt around it. In design the brolly was not, of course, as it is now, but only had, at the most, a 45in rib, and the majority in use were less: some were of only 36in.

The first that was practical as a bivvie was the one sold by Send Marketing. Very simple to use, the brolly was just planted upright and the cover made from canvas draped over. When pegged it was surprisingly robust, and done properly, it would stand quite a big wind. The one major drawback it had is that so-called friends could, in the small hours, unpeg it and spin it through 180 degrees, re-peg it and sound off the alarms. The resultant mayhem can easily be imagined. There was a plethora of designs, but at that time just about all were based around the umbrella. Probably the most useful of these was the idea of what became known as 'storm sides'. These bivvies were really practical, and stayed in wide use until quite recently.

The mid-seventies saw a definite decline in the fishing at Sywell; tiny bites at very infrequent intervals made us look elsewhere. More 7lb fish were being reported

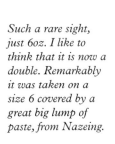

Such a rare sight, just 6oz. I like to think that it is now a double. Remarkably it was taken on a size 6 covered by a great big lump of paste, from Nazeing.

123

nationally, and I was still desperate for one, as was Janet. Along with a group of friends, we started fishing locally to my home, at the northern end of the Lee Valley.

We caught fish immediately, not big nationally, but worthwhile nevertheless, with quite a few at 5lb to 6lb. We decided to stick to the valley for a while and see what we could catch. I bought myself a couple of carbon blanks, my first ones. At 12ft and 1¼lb test curve, they were a revelation, light and responsive. I loved them and used them until they became just too soft to use in a big headwind. Along with the change of rod material, I changed to

Roger Smith at Nazeing, an excellent illustration of the quality of fishing at that time. The best fish were around 5lb or so.

centred rings. The ones I used were the lightweight Hopkins and Holloway design, very similar to the French Chromex that I had used for decades. A very nice touch with those blanks was that they came with a ready-fitted spigot joint, which saved a lot of fiddling about.

As an aside to the above, I always used spigotted rods. We all, I hope, fish for pleasure, and a little of that pleasure is in the tackle one uses. The idea of rods that are all sorts of different diameter in the middle I find just a bit aesthetically displeasing. I was once told by a well-respected rod builder that I could not tell the difference if blindfolded. That I most certainly agree with; however, I don't fish blindfolded, just cast like I am sometimes.

My Seven-Pounder

I did eventually get a seven-pounder, from the centre Lagoon at Nazeing. It came out of the blue at lunchtime on a lovely sunny day, a cracking-looking fish, a milestone for us. Needless to say it was not the start of a flood of monsters, and it was the end of the following summer before I had another. The year that I caught it, Roger Smith, who was fishing with us at the time, showed us something that was to prove pivotal. The object was a little smaller than a golf ball, hard and round: 'I got it from secret Len [Arbury],' he said, 'It's what they are getting them on down on Johnsons, loads of big uns.' The first sight of a boilie: what on earth does one do with the thing?

After the initial excitement, no one could figure it out, and it was quite some time before we found out how it was done. When we did, we took it to Homersfield and really caught a lot of carp. But it was fun, and it gave us all a springboard to head off in other directions if we wanted; most of us stayed in the Lee Valley fishing

The best I had from Nazeing, 7lb 14oz, a beautiful late season fish. Probably the most satisfying tench that I have caught.

for tench, but Roger went off to Savay where he and the late Bob Jones did great things; and Janet, Rob Brace and I went to fish Stanstead Abbotts, the big pit. At that time it was, like just about everywhere else, being fished conventionally, with maggots, paste, worms – all the usual things.

I had a carrier bag of boilies left over from a trip to Homersfield. Once we had decided on an area to fish, we catapulted the lot into it. And just for a change, it all came right, and we all caught a lot of fish. There were no big ones, just a fair number of 5lb fish and a few six-pounders, but quite busy fishing. We just could not get enough of it, and I seemed to spend most of my time making bait. The whole process was just so laborious: we didn't have any

aids at all, no bait rollers or bait guns; the only thing we had that helped was a Kenwood Chef mixer – and I still use it now for bait making. In the interests of domestic harmony we purchased another one to be used purely for human food! Gardner Tackle eventually solved all our problems with a range of bait rollers in different sizes, culminating in the one I currently use, which makes about eighty baits for one pass of the slider. There were not many ready-made baits on the market, and to a great extent we all had to make our own, though there were some dry ingredients to be had; in particular, big Rod Hutchinson was introducing some really good ones, most of which are still catching fish today.

A brace of sevens before breakfast, Larkfield, July 1988. Amazingly the water is, at the time of writing, producing double-figure males as well as females.

One of the 'Catchum' range with which I caught fish was the seafood mix that caught me a one-time personal best at 7lb 14oz from Nazeing. A late-season fish, it was very impressive, and Roger Smith made an excellent job of the pictures.

For a few years we had often said at the start of a trip, 'a brace of seven-pounders before breakfast and then we can get serious!' Though we had seen a few 7lb fish, the reality of a brace had, until the late seventies and into the early eighties, just seemed a pipe dream. The only ones that we had known of with any degree of certainty was the then amazing catch that Len Head had made from Bures, which re-wrote the tench-fishing history books.

Stanstead Abbotts, though good, was not giving the impression of being able to deliver the goods. The lake was producing some very big carp, but not tench. And so it was travelling again for us, this time off to Kent and Larkfield, as there were rumours of some very big fish, reputedly 9lb or more. We would take the magic boilies to see what we could do on a water

126

that we understood had already had some experience of them. As luck would have it, the weather was very hot and we absolutely sweltered the whole time that we were there. But we did catch some big fish: both Janet and I had seven-pounders, and I had the magic brace of sevens – where to next, I wondered.

BACK TO SYWELL

Within the space of only three or four years, tench had vastly increased in size, and by the late eighties and early nineties fish of 7lb to 9lb or so hardly raised an eyebrow. By 1989, word was coming through of remarkable catches from Sywell, and given that nationally there were a lot of big fish being caught, the water was doing surprising things. Hearing about multiple catches of 7lb and 8lb fish and the odd nine-pounder thrown in, we had to have some of the action – so Janet and I went to Northamptonshire again.

What a difference we found from when we had first fished there. Gone was the peace and solitude, and in its place an endless stream of incomers from the greatly enlarged Northampton and Wellingborough towns. Some people would spend their time running round the place, all sweat bands and stop watches, intent on going round three seconds faster than the

First chuck, a 7lb 6oz. Janet saw me off that day.

day before. But the worst offenders were the dogs, their owners bringing them to habitually defecate on the path with no regard for those people who followed them. Joe King, the water engineer who for so many years had nurtured and loved the place, was gone: rather than be evicted from the place he loved, he had shot himself. Somebody somewhere has, I hope, a twinge of conscience over that.

The day we arrived the weather was rough, with rain and a brisk breeze blowing, as ever, from the middle of the lake outwards. Wherever one fished, the wind was in your face! With little hope or expectation, we set up at the cow-shed swim, the big beds of bulrush affording a little shelter from the driving rain. I catapulted out about a hundred or so baits in both swims, and, shivering under brollies, we awaited a reaction. It was not long in coming. Janet's Mitchell reel began to spin madly, she struck, and the rod took on a goodly battle curve, a bit of lug and tug and the fish was in the net. Immediately it was weighed we both felt a good deal warmer because it was 7lb 6oz, a very good start.

That was the first of half-a-dozen seven-pounders we had that afternoon, Janet having the lion's share, with four of them. Needless to say we were back again the following day, with a similar result, but with the honours more evenly spread. For a while we split our time between local waters and Sywell: we were still chasing that so far elusive eight-pounder.

THE WATER HOLE

One water that we spent a bit of time on was a fairly large one where some big fish had been seen. Known locally as the Water Hole, it is, I suppose, just that, roughly rectangular and without a great deal of feature. There was just a couple of substantial bars and, interestingly, the sunken framework of a building, the concrete frame appearing above the surface in times of drought. On that water I finally got my eight-pounder, long awaited and chased all over the country, and then caught on a water just ten minutes from home. To say I was pleased would be a

At 8lb 2oz, my first 8lb fish. Like most of the Lea Valley, the fish are even bigger now.

gross understatement. A small group of us persisted with it, but only one other eight-pounder was caught, and that was a rather bizarre capture. Rob Brace, friend and fellow tench catcher of many years, was fishing with us and I saw him strike into a fish. The rod duly bent over, giving all the signs of a good fish – which it must have been, as line was even pulled off against the clutch. After a little while he had the better of it and his lead appeared on the surface, no sign of the fish, but it was only on a short hook-length – very strange.

A float became visible just below the lead, and the boilie appeared – but still no sign of a fish. He kept at it; he had the lead almost in the tip ring, and then the fish swirled on the surface and we duly netted it. Quite remarkably, it had earlier broken somebody and was then towing the length of line with the float attached until it fouled Rob's line. He then played it as if it were directly hooked on a size 6 and 6lb line. In reality, he was attached to it via 3lb line and a size 14!

As ever, we caught carp there, though not particularly big, mid-doubles mostly. They brightened up days when nothing much was doing; other than that they were, as on a lot of other waters that we fished, a bit of a nuisance at times.

In the end we left the Water Hole and concentrated on Sywell, a move that paid dividends, as we had some wonderful fishing of the very highest quality. The fish just seemed to get bigger as the seasons went on, and in the end we almost lost count of the eight-pounders we had caught, and became blasé about it all.

Tackle and Baits

The end tackle we used was really simple, as ever, just 8lb Maxima, straight through to a size 6 or a size 8 hook. I started off using Drennan boilie hooks with the barbs crushed down as far as I possibly could; I have never been a great fan of barbed hooks, and even now only use them for worm fishing, or in small sizes for maggots. Quite often, however, one can use small slivers of elastic to keep maggots on. Later, Janet and I changed to Drennan Starpoints, a really excellent hook that Len Arbury put us on to at a group meeting. I have used them ever since, and for tench of any size they are the best hook I have ever used. But no doubt there are others that I have yet to see and use.

Recipe for Disaster

For a couple of seasons we enjoyed, as I said earlier, great fishing. We then started to get the odd damaged fish, with maybe a torn mouth, or lips torn off, really horrible injuries. At first there was no clear indication as to how this was happening, but as we took more interest in what others were doing, there started to be clues as to how this awfulness was being caused. Firstly, a lot of people were using braided hook-lengths, something that if used in a reasonable manner, should do little harm. But that was coupled to lines in excess of 10lb breaking strain, which have little or no place in the tench-fishing scene, because using such material is an almost irresistible invitation to use it to its full potential.

In the middle of the year, tench spend a lot of time in often very dense weed, particularly at spawning time. At Sywell, the fish regularly gathered quite long distances from the bank in small holes in the weed, and the method that some anglers had evolved to fish these areas was simple: they used the aforesaid heavy reel line, at least 15lb breaking strain, and a braid hook-length. Couple that with a 2oz, 3oz or even 4oz fixed lead – and there you have it, a recipe for disaster. I watched on a number of occasions the 'playing technique'

Always fish into the wind: a gentle breeze at Sywell.

employed with this tackle: rod over the shoulder, and walk away from the water. Either the line broke leaving the fish tethered, or it was hauled out in a great ball of weed.

This behaviour was totally irresponsible, and something had to be done to prevent further damage. On the face of it, the solution was a good try: that of float fishing only. Admittedly this was, as always, rather at the mercy of the elements, since a big wind would make the place all but unfishable with float gear – in fact the very condi-

tions that were often really productive, the rougher the better. Fishing in such weather it was obvious that some would bend the rules, and all manner of ridiculous end tackles were chucked in, so that within a season or so, the problem was almost as bad as before. I had long before decided that I wanted none of this nonsense, and was looking elsewhere – although really it was a shame, because the fishing was of the highest order: both Janet and I caught fish of 9lb or more, and an inordinate amount of 7lb-plus fish.

Wherever we went, the fish had to be big: the idea of fishing for four- or five-pounders as a target did not appeal. The Lea Valley was, by the early nineties, producing some of the sort of fish that we were looking for, right from Walthamstow to Ware, not only the stillwaters, but the river as well. So why were all these extraordinary fish turning up? In just about any water that contained a good quality population not only of tench, but bream as well, the fish were really piling on the pounds. Unfortunately the carp scene was to some extent open to misinterpretation because of widespread illicit or downright illegal importation. Even so, there was still a general increase in the average size. Why this should be, I haven't a definitive answer, and the best guess would have to be global warming. Nevertheless, I do think that there are other factors involved, and widespread chemically induced sterility and sex change are other factors that should be put into the equation.

That the average temperature has increased there is no doubt, and for what it is worth, my own view is that the temperature rise in winter is far more important than the summer temperature. That would allow both fish, insect and invertebrate life to be active for longer – indeed, there are probably only a couple of months or so when there is not a realistic chance of tench feeding. I know that there is a theory in some quarters that bait is a factor, and on just a few waters it may be so, but in general I think that most big fish get that way without outside interference. I know of one or two waters that thrived on neglect, never seeing a boilie, yet still produced big ones.

A LOCAL WATER

Between trips to Sywell, for some time we had been trying a local water. Neglected for a long time, it had first come to our attention when a friend told us of a 7lb-plus tench he had caught. Sporadic trips produced very little, my first season on it producing just one fish, about 4½lb – not a very good or promising start. The following year I found little better until late September, when I landed a seven-pounder.

Persisting with the bait and method we had been so successful with at Sywell, very slowly the tide turned and we started getting fish in the following seasons, and a few good ones, too: 7lb and 8lb fish were fairly regular, though not as often as at Sywell. The water is very irregular, both in overall shape and also in its underwater contour, so there are many places for fish to get to. The other factor in making the place such a challenge is the low population density. They often totally forsake whole chunks of the water for days on end, and are hidden away in near-inaccessible stretches, which makes the whole fishing process hard work at times.

The decade moved on, and the fish just got bigger and bigger. I thought there was a chance that somebody would get that coveted 10lb fish, as there had been a number in excess of 9lb, and some very close to the magic 10lb. I was full of hope: I had missed by 2 or 3oz on a couple of occasions – surely I would be in with a chance.

Then in 1998 Janet's and my personal world fell apart when I was diagnosed with leukaemia, a very big shock. A long course of treatment followed that kept me off the bank for a good while, its debilitating effects pushing all thought of fishing far back in the consciousness. In late 1999 I did make just four trips out, though in truth I was not really up to it, and I needed the help of my guardian angel to do anything, really. But the new millennium was different, and I was able to

MORE ON BAIT

set to with a will. We made a load of bait, enough for at least half a season, and I started fishing.

One thing I would like to enlarge on is the subject of bait. There is a tremendous amount written about it, so why should I not add to it? There are absolutely hundreds of flavours that can be used, some better than others, some inexplicably a complete failure. It can be of absorbing interest to explore what there is and its effect on one's fishing, but there is a caveat to it, in that one can be led, sometimes literally, by the nose down blind alleys. A far better option is to use proven flavours, those with a good track record, though admittedly it is tempting to want to try new ones. Indeed I do it myself

A lovely 9lb 7oz fish taken at the beginning of June 2005.

A splendid 8lb 14oz fish that was caught in late autumn 2003.

occasionally: whatever it is, it might be the next wonder bait.

The same criterion applies to base mixes: once you have a base that fits the parameters you lay down for your fishing, then try to stick to it, though by all means juggle the percentages within it. There are two things to remember: first, keep it simple – it is all too easy to fall into the trap of confusing yourself with unnecessary science. By all means learn what the constituent parts of your bait are, but just remember that nutrition is a very complex science, and we are still learning about what we consume ourselves. With regard to fish, the surface is hardly more than

133

scratched. Keep in mind that even the best bait in the world can fail sometimes, and you experience a blank, or even a succession of blanks. This does not mean that no fish will ever eat it again; more likely you are having a crisis of confidence with what you are using.

Finally, a lot of fish of several species are taken on Tutti-Frutti boilies every year. Unless you are very lucky with what is in your bag, the nutritional value of what is on the hair is little more than a handful of grass.

A TRIP TO CASTLE LAKE

It was late April 2000, and the first trip of the year: once again we set off to Castle Lake. After all the rigmarole of setting up, making a mental note to collect the various things I had forgotten, I finally cast out, catapulting out a couple of dozen freebies. Late evening and a bobbin shot up, a solid strike and a good fish on; a bit of to-ing and fro-ing and it was in the net. It was quickly unhooked and left in the landing net while preparations for weighing were sorted out. The first job was to screw a hook into a tree, a trick I had first used several years before. Suspending a balance from a hook in this manner made viewing the balance so much easier, with no pointer rattling up and down, and the balance hanging truly vertically. Done in this way, there is no outside influence on the result; it is all too easy to put a finger on the casing to try and steady it, which has great potential for influencing the reading.

I put the tench in the weigh sling and on to the balance hook, and the pointer went down and down until it rested on 9lb 6oz plus the bag weight: a cracking start. Over the next couple of days there followed a succession of decent fish, 7lb or 8lb and another of 9lb 3oz. For the next few weeks there were a number of good fish, 7lb and 8lb mostly, with the odd small fish just to keep my feet on the ground.

MY FIRST TEN-POUNDER

The end of May into the beginning of June was, for me, a really remarkable time, a spell when not only did I get the longed for ten-pounder, it was in the company of three eight-pounders and two nine-pounders – and one of the eight-pounders was just an ounce short of nine. Though the weight dropped a little after spawning, they don't carry a great deal. Weights by the autumn were, on average, within 6oz or so of their weight in late spring.

The rest of the season had no more surprises, a few blanks, a few fish. The water has never been busy, just one or two bites a day, though often not even that. Certainly it was not like Sywell where one cast out, not with the thought, 'Am I going to get a bite?' but more likely, 'How many am I going to get today?'

Looking at my diary entries for that year, I stopped catching at the beginning of October, ending with quite a reasonable final fish of 7lb 10oz. All in all this was a really good year, and a personal best was just the icing on the cake.

THE MYSTERY FISH

Over the next two or three seasons the fishing was quite good, but gave the impression of having reached some sort of plateau as far as weight was concerned. Certainly there wasn't much sign of any bigger fish than those that had visited the bank already. I was, however, outwitted by a fish that was out of the ordinary – and it wasn't a carp. The unknown fish displayed no desire to go boring off at high speed, as

A superb 9lb 14oz fish caught in early April 2002.

most carp do, and there was no blind panic; for a while it just plodded along, holding a long way out, not doing much. Then it just swam away, getting a little faster as it went. It ended up in very dense flannel weed, where it broke the line.

The only other time I experienced anything like this was an occasion at Sywell when a mystery fish behaved in exactly the same way, ending up in dense flannel where it easily broke 8lb line. But that sort of thing is part of the stuff of angling: a little bit of mystery, what could it be: was it a tench? If so, was it foul hooked, or was it worthy of Colonel Thornton? I love the latter idea, but it is much more likely to be the former, just a good fish hooked at the wrong end of the digestive system.

That apart, through that period I had something approaching fifty tench of 8lb or more, the best an ounce or two under the new magic weight of 10lb. Quite good fishing!

WHAT FISHING IS ALL ABOUT

A long time ago, Richard Walker quoted a passage by Rudyard Kipling: 'The calculated craftsmanship that camps alone

135

before the angry rifle pit or shell hole and cleanly and methodically wipes out every soul in it.' He (RW) said 'you've got to be deadly.' After many years of trying to be deadly, that sort of thing tends to pall a bit, and I drifted away from it a long time ago. The companionship of a group of friends becomes more important than before, and reasonably often a fishing trip is more of a social affair: a barbecue, some bottles of wine, talk of fishing past, or planning future trips. As Roger Smith would say, 'This is what fishing is all about.'

As time has gone on, food has become more of a priority, particularly when staying over for several days. I have always enjoyed food, and am quite prepared to go to some trouble over it, taking ingredients and preparing it on the bank. The other option is that Janet prepares food at home and it is reheated or cooked on the bank, one of the joys of living five minutes from where one is fishing. This was christened 'meals on wheels' by Rob Brace.

A final aside on the subject of food: nationally we have a problem of some magnitude with crayfish, yet for very little effort they can be caught, cooked and eaten with a plate of pasta and a rather nice sauce. Why not? It's better than stamping on them and throwing them in the bushes.

Just about up to the present day, 2004 to 2005, there was more brilliant fishing, possibly not good enough for people to search for my rod-rest holes, but pretty good, nevertheless. There has been a good stack of 8lb and 9lb fish, and a ten-pounder as well, an excellent year.

Looking back over all this has been, in a way, a bit of an adventure: re-living what I have caught, the places I have been to, and above all, the people I have met and those I have fished with. And the fishing itself has all along has been a transport of delight, from three-, four- and five-pounders of long ago Southill to the present day, and monsters of ten pounds and more.

Would I do it all again? You bet I would! I only have to look down on another golden-flanked fish, and the magic flares again.

5 Big Tench Fanatic

by Dave Harman

GIANT TENCH, FIRST ENCOUNTERS

In early July 1985 I found myself on the banks of Ferris Meadow fishing for tench and bream, the size of which I had only dreamt about. Hours into that first session I had been snapped up twice on light float tackle by good tench. A week later I landed my first tench from there, a new personal best by an ounce at 4lb 3oz; and the love affair began.

On the 15 June 1986 I was settled into a small point swim all ready for action: by 9.30am the next morning, after losing a very big tench on a feeder, I landed a beast of 8lb 3oz on the float. During the rest of the season I lost two more tench – but the place had me hooked.

The 1987 season was unbelievable for me. A personal best bream of 7lb 14oz and a 6lb 14oz tench were taken on the first day from the small point. Then the next trip to the 'Beach' gave me three 5lb-plus tench in the evening, before an outstanding morning session, when between 4.20am and 12.30pm I landed six tench and two bream, the biggest two tench weighing 8lb 11oz and an enormous 9lb 12oz. To put that into context for any younger readers, the biggest fish reported so far that season was a 9lb 10oz specimen to the 'man himself', Alan Wilson from Tring.

I ended the season with twenty-seven fish, which wasn't bad for eight days' fishing! I didn't drive at the time, and would be dropped off and collected by taxis, booked in advance. Nights were spent kipping on a deckchair with only a plastic mackintosh for cover (no night fishing at the time), and hot food was not on the menu. But such was the effect the place had on me, nothing was too much trouble.

The following year brought me sharply back down to earth, however, with just a 4lb male for the season. Then in 1989 Jackie Davis joined, bringing with him transport. We shared our knowledge, and slowly we learned the lake's secrets. Later that year Rory Adair joined, and managed a good tench on his first trip.

As the years progressed good friends were made and many good fish landed, with a handful over 9lb. Unfortunately with these successes came competition, and soon it became apparent that fishing sociably and catching equal amounts of fish seldom went together.

By the end of June 1992 the atmosphere had changed, with everyone supposedly cutting off each other's fish. Each successive year had only delivered one tench topping my personal best of 9lb 12oz, the largest a fish of exactly 10lb, caught at the start of this season, so I decided to venture onto pastures new. And so the travelling began.

June 1990: early success in the form of a 7lb 6oz Ferris Meadow specimen.

THE QUEST BEGINS

The spring of 1993 was spent checking out new pits in search of that elusive 'double'. I wanted a water near to home that gave me the opportunity to bait a swim in preparation for the glorious 16 June. This was a scary experience, leaving the safety of Ferris where I knew I could catch a few good fish, to venture out to somewhere new. By early May I had a shortlist of three venues: Wraysbury 2, Kingsmead and Sheepwalk. To be honest the Sheepwalk was looking favourite, as it was only four miles from home, and the sheer size of the other two venues was daunting, especially for a very proud young man who wouldn't accept failure lightly.

Then one day I was out on the tree in the corner, near the kennels on Kingsmead, watching a few 5lb to 6lb tench milling about and the odd carp drifting in, when I spotted the biggest tench I have ever seen. A fish caught my eye near the far bank, then it turned and headed towards me just under the surface. From the length and the width it appeared to be an upper double carp, but as it came through, no more than three feet below me and just under the surface, I could see clearly that it was a tench of incredible proportions! I wouldn't want to put a weight on it, as I didn't get a decent view of its depth, but from the length and thickness across its back it must have been at least 14lb.

The decision had been made for me, and after several trips with the plumbing rod, a swim was selected near the bridge and a three-week baiting campaign began. Never before had I so eagerly awaited the start of a new season, and after moving into a new house on 13 June, I could contain myself no longer.

Straight from work on the 14th, I grabbed my tackle and raced round to my swim, more than a little relieved to find it empty. I set up my bivvy, baited the swim, then had just finished dinner when the head bailiff arrived and told me I had to leave! Apparently you weren't allowed on until 9am on the 15th, but when I asked if my swim would be free then, he said he didn't know.

As I made the two trips back to the car, I don't know whether I was more angry or despondent and I nearly ended up back at Ferris. In the end, I was back at Kingsmead at 5am. With my tackle hidden in the bushes near my swim, I patrolled the bridge awaiting the arrival of the other anglers. But 9am eventually arrived, and I still had the place to myself, and not long after I was settled back into my swim anticipating what lay ahead. By the afternoon heavy rain had set in and I had a nice flow of water running through my bivvy; but nothing could dampen my spirits.

Eventually midnight came and two swim-feeders splashed into position; then one hopeful angler sat on his bedchair, sleep far from his mind. Thirty minutes later I missed a drop-back, then just after 1am an eel of about 2lb graced the net. When the bobbin rose slowly to the top an hour later I suspected another, but was quite pleased when it turned out to be a bream of 8lb 9oz, followed shortly after by one of 5lb.

Dawn came, and the rain cleared away. As I watched the pit, occasionally fish would roll over both my baited areas. I had a few re-casts, then at 5.40am the right rod roared into life and what was obviously a tench was giving my 6lb line a run for its money. Eventually I was weighing her, and at 6lb 10oz, she was a reasonable start. Then an hour later a 4lb male picked up the maggots on the other rod.

The day was uneventful until 4pm, when another 4lb male came along. It was a promising start, and at least I had caught a few fish on a new water. I baited again that evening and retired to bed at dusk, tired from lack of sleep.

At 2.40am the bream arrived, and by the time they departed at 9am, I had taken six of them up to 7lb 6oz. The day was uneventful, with the final night producing just one bream. No other tench were caught during my visit; all the other anglers were fishing for carp, and had barely caught a tench between them in many seasons.

With the vision of the leviathan I saw in the spring still fresh in my mind, I spent the next three weeks trying different areas; but apart from the occasional bream and eels, my trips remained unrewarded. Finally come mid-July I wanted to catch some tench, and having bought a group ticket, I decided I would have a trip to Larkfield 2 in Kent, on advice from another angler.

On arrival at Larkfield 2, I was amazed to find the place overrun with carp anglers, such was my naïvity at the time. They were friendly enough with advice and even an offer of breakfast, but as I stared at the almost empty banks of Johnson's Railway Lake, something inside told me my future lay there.

The Railway Lake is a magical place steeped in history and atmosphere, and with the writings of 'Gibbo' and 'Turnbull' fresh in my mind, I wandered its banks with a rod and a lead in search of a starting point. As I reached the end of the road bank, I met a carp angler called 'Two Bob' who suggested a couple of areas in the willows on the railway bank. I wished him well and went about my business. The weed was unbelievable, and it wasn't until I reached a small dug-out swim near the end of the bank that I found a few clear areas.

I quickly dragged my tackle down there and set up two two-hook feeder rigs. I then rolled up forty balls of groundbait laced with hemp, wheat and cockles (on advice), and deposited twenty on to each of the two spots. One spot about fifty yards out appeared to be in excess of fifteen feet; the other, only about thirty yards out, felt about ten feet deep. Once sorted, I went back to the car for a last couple of bits and arrived at 'Two Bobs' swim just in time to net the lake's biggest resident for him, 'The Leather', at over 32lb; I took a few photos, and a friend was made.

It was a pleasant evening, and I settled into my swim and had a few re-casts; when my left buzzer screamed into life, I leapt from my chair like a man possessed. After a dogged fight in the weedy water a good tench was in the net; at just over 8lb, I was well pleased. I popped her in a sack and ran down to fetch 'Two Bob' for the photos.

I retired at about 11pm after watching the lake go to bed; it already had a grip on me, and I knew I would be enjoying this view many more times. Then at 3am I was woken up by a sort of yo-yo style bite, which I suspected was a bream; upon hitting it, however, a strong resistance was felt. Slowly I gained line, but then all went solid; I pumped the rod in an effort to cut through the weed with my line, and eventually got it moving. Soon a huge clump of weed broke surface accompanied by the odd fish-like swirl; but I only had a 30in net. In the end I had to wrestle the weedbed into the net, and then, still not sure as to what I had caught, I took it up to my bivvy for inspection. As I pulled at the weed a thick slimy tail wrapped round my arm and it became apparent that a large eel had picked up the cockles. After unhooking her, I coaxed her into my weigh sling, and at 4lb 4oz she was a new personal best by over 1½lb. Well pleased, I popped her in a sack, and an hour later two carp anglers, who dropped into the neighbouring swims, took some photos for me.

Early morning gave me two bream to 8lb 2oz on bread, and a missed one noter, then the action died off. I was getting to like it here more every minute. After an early night I was dragged from my pit at 11.15pm by what felt like a good tench; but it dived in the weed, eventually breaking the hook-length. The following morning came and passed, and by lunchtime I was unwillingly hauling my tackle back to the car, already eagerly anticipating my return.

Three days later I was back on a sixty-hour session, this time arriving pre-dawn; after watching a few tench rolling in a swim on the road bank, I elected to fish there. There was a clear area about twenty feet deep and half the size of a tennis court, surrounded on all sides by weed growing almost to the surface, which appeared to be the only fishable water in the swim. Never having caught tench in such deep water I was a little dubious, but decided to try it, anyway. Two areas tight to the weed wall were given twenty balls of groundbait each, followed by the usual two-hook feeder rigs; then I sat and waited.

The morning passed, and I was thinking I had made a bad choice, when at 12.15pm the left rod roared into life; after a lively battle in the open water I soon had a reasonable tench in the net. At 7lb 1oz it had fought well for its size; its tail was 7in deep, which probably explained its power.

The day had been warm, and as I settled down to cook some dinner at 9.15pm I lost a fish, after it appeared to cut through the hook-length. Then all was quiet until 1.15am when a 7lb 11oz bream took a liking to the cockles, which so far the tench hadn't.

I was up at dawn to see plenty of tench rolling in my swim, but it wasn't until 8.40am that I missed the first run. This seemed to start a run of bad luck (or ignorance), because over the rest of the trip I lost all six fish that I hooked, either to hook pulls or breakages; so I christened the swim 'The Not Allowed'. The final nail in the coffin came when the exhaust fell off the car on the M25 on the way home.

A week later I was back, this time with Rory who was keen to catch a few tench. We arrived on Saturday evening after I had finished work, and it was 9pm by the time we had settled in the 'High Bank' swim, on the causeway bank. At 6.45am I had my first – and last – tench on a cockle, at 5lb 10oz. It had red dots all over it (this was the first time I had ever seen a tench like it) so we christened it 'Rik Pem' after a spotty youth of yesteryear. The day was uneventful, but at least Rory met a few of the angling characters on the many pits there.

By mid-morning on the last day we had still had no action, so Rory tried something different. He set up a weightless feeder on a long paternoster, and fished casters on to the weed. Over the remaining few hours he landed five tench, the best 8lb ½oz, 24in long, and spawn free.

With Rory now hooked as well, we fished through to the end of September, getting to know the pit and a few of its inhabitants. Rory's initial success seemed to be short-lived, as the few tench he caught were mainly small; however, I managed to land several more tench, including three over 8lb, a personal best male of 6lb 12oz, and the lake's second-largest resident carp at the time, a strange-looking mirror of 31lb 9oz known as 'The Prehistoric'. To say we couldn't wait for the following June was an understatement.

Two weeks before the 1994 season began, Rory and I were inspecting and baiting the Railway Lake with a newly purchased dinghy. An early morning arrival had again drawn our attention to the 'Not Allowed' swim, dominating the dawn rolling action. We baited the whole of the area that had been clear last season, but was now surprisingly weedy, and left the fish to do the work.

A week later we did the same, and the area already felt considerably clearer. At 3am on the 15th we pulled up behind our swim and were greeted by a multitude of rolling fish; with no rush to ready our tackle we sat and enjoyed the spectacle, knowing that the next day we would be pulling them in for sure. The bottom, when we plumbed it, was clear! By evening the pit was nigh on full, with most people socializing in our swim, especially interested as the carp ate their way through 4kg of chum mixers. Midnight approached, and everyone made their way to their respective swims, eager to get the rods out.

By now we were fishing four rods each, and after last year's punishment on 6lb line, had stepped up to 8lb. As the clock struck midnight, our first cast of the season was made – and before I had baited my third rod, the first took off at such a frightening pace I barely dared to bend into it. It tore line from the spool for a few seconds, and then was gone: the hook-length had parted! I stood there shaking, not at all ready for what had just occurred. I had redesigned my feeders with the lead bulked near the swivel, hoping to improve the bolt effect, and it had certainly done that! I guessed one of the carp had taken a liking to my casters.

Rory had a 7lb bream at about 2am, and so I was able to christen my new landing net; then at about 8am he lost a tench of about 6lb at the net. There was no more action until 3.30pm, when I pulled out of a good tench, after another amazing run. Then at 6pm a repeat performance saw the swim live up to its name. Enough was enough, and I changed to 13lb Silcast mainline, 15lb braided hook-length and a size 8 Super Specialist hook.

During the night Rory had another bream, then at dawn he yelled he was into a tench; but as I went to net it, it turned into a good eel. I netted it first time, but was then flabbergasted to see it reappear behind the net, with his line running through it: something had obviously eaten the bream slime and holed it. I tried to grab the eel, but it shot backwards through my hand, thankfully not snagging me with the second hook. Rory pulled it back towards the net, and somehow I managed to flick it back over the rim and rush it up the bank. It had been an eventful way to wake up, and Rory was pleased with a new personal best of 3lb 11oz.

The day gave me 'Rik Pem', up in weight at 6lb 2oz with some spawn, and another tench of 6lb 8oz, both on casters. The weather was frying, and the day was spent hiding under brollies. The following day was the same, and no action befell either of us; no carp had been caught, or any other tench landed. In the space of a few days the pit had turned lifeless.

Dawn on the 19th gave me a personal best eel of 4lb 5oz, and one of the carp anglers, 'Mad Steve', popped round; he had landed a 10lb 1oz tench that we went to admire. Then early the following morning Jackie Davis came down for a visit, with the news that Ferris had gone crazy. Out of ten tench landed so far, there had been two different fish of 11lb 8oz, and five others of over 9lb. It was hard to take in; the previous year Ferris had produced its first double at 10lb on the dot, and it had never produced more than four 9lb-plus tench in a season.

Not long after, however, one of my rods ripped into life; but after a good fight I was a little disappointed to see a 13lb pike slide into the landing net. But soon after I was in again, the heavy plodding signalling a good tench. After what seemed like an eternity, Rory slipped the net under it, and as we prepared the scales we wondered what it might weigh. On the scales it weighed in at 9lb 13oz, and I was well pleased; it was a new personal best by an ounce, and seven years in the waiting.

Over the next two days I had a couple of males, including a new personal best of 7lb 9oz; but Rory remained without a bite, and moved swim for the remaining two days. The sun was relentless, and most of the fish in the lake were holed up under a tree. Deep down I could see two huge tench tails, and after a constant flow of rotten casters salvaged from Rory's rubbish bag, two tench, both over 11lb, eventually joined in the activity. The swim was tight at best, but with the top half of a 2½lb rod with a reel taped on, 13lb line straight through to a size 6 hook baited with four casters, I thought I had a fair chance.

Carefully drawing my bait away from the many large carp present, I eventually got one of the two big tench to take my bait off a sunken twig, just below the surface. All hell broke loose when I struck, with the

June 1994: a fish of 9lb 13oz from Johnson's Railway Lake – a new personal best, seven years in the waiting.

hook straightening whilst trying to keep the tench from the branches. An hour later I successfully extracted a 7lb 1oz male from the swim – by which time the fish had had enough, and left.

One more of 5lb 4oz brought the session to an end, and on my return a week later most of the tench were busy spawning. So I had a couple of trips to Ferris and bagged a couple over 9lb, and a few more good ones. I also made a brief visit to Johnson's Road/Island Lake, where in twenty-six hours I managed to land twenty-seven tench, the best a 7lb 1oz

143

male, with twenty-two of the fish coming on the second morning. It was total bedlam, and I also probably lost four or five fish on the several occasions that I had two fish on at once. All three baited patches went crazy, and by the time I left I ached for two days.

A couple of trips back on the Railway later in the year produced a few more good tench up to 8lb 15oz; but the size of the Ferris beasts and a couple of new friends, Chris Sullivan and Warren Hammond, would draw us back to Ferris for the start of the 1995 season.

EUPHORIA OR NOT?

In the spring of 1995 the closed season on stillwaters was abandoned, and so Rory, Chris, Warren and I descended on the banks of Larkfield 2. Here, after only a couple of trips, we began the 'monster baiting' routine. It was quite apparent that the venue held a lot of tench of all sizes, and with anglers fishing and baiting most of the swims on a daily basis, we thought it would be worth our while to make our swim more appealing than the others. As the sessions progressed, so the volume of bait and number of fish caught increased, until eventually most sessions began with an initial bombardment of 300 balls of groundbait, often taking five hours to make and catapult, a back-breaking task.

Unfortunately Larkfield never gave us a 'double', although we had a lot over 9lb; the best was 9lb 15oz to Rory, his first nine-pounder. But for sheer numbers of fish it was incredible: my best night gave me more than thirty runs, not bad on a water where the locals didn't expect to get that in a season!

At last 5 June arrived, and so desperate was I for a 'double' that I was already camped on Ferris in the 'Pier Swim', with

three marker floats out and bait going in regularly. As the days passed, my swim looked more and more promising, with more tench activity daily, until a couple of days from the off when everyone started arriving. But all the plumbing and baiting had a negative effect on the pit, rendering it almost lifeless.

By the evening of the 15th the pit was nearly full: Rory and Chris were in the 'Beach' on the opposite bank, with the 'Cheeses' nearby in the 'Shed'. Next to me was Warren, followed by Larry Sprucen and Jim Cheverall, and then a few of the 'Tench Fishers'; so a good evening was had by all, and it was not until after half-past midnight that my rods were eventually cast out.

Dawn came and we crawled from our bivvies; Chris had a bream during the night, but it was not until 8am that I pulled the first tench of the season from the lake, at 5lb 4oz. A 9lb bream to Jim Cheverall in the mid-afternoon finalized the action for opening day.

During the second night Rory managed one of the elusive carp, a little under 20lb, and a couple of bream were caught; then shortly after 9am, having just landed a bream, Chris Sullivan dragged out a monster tench, so we all raced round to the 'Beach'. At 10lb 14oz it was the biggest tench we had seen – and only Chris could have managed to catch it with both hooks in its mouth! later that afternoon I managed one of 8lb 6oz.

The next day gave me a 9lb 3oz fish that I was well pleased with; and Chris lost a good one after tying his rods together. A handful of fish were landed over the next two days between us, but nothing of note, and I must admit I was done in, each day passing seemingly narrowing the odds of my 'double'.

At 2.45am the next morning I was woken to be told that Rory had landed a

June 1995: 10lb 14oz, and Chris Sullivan living up to his catchphrase 'that's another one caught on a feeder'.

tench weighing an almost unbelievable 12lb ½oz. The lake was alive, and everyone went round to see it. Except me! Pleased as I was for Rory, I felt my chance of a double had gone, and I drifted back into sleep at an all-time low. Sleep came fitfully, proba- bly because I knew I had disgraced myself amongst good friends; looking back, I know the reason for my behaviour was because I felt I was entitled to the first 'double', having caught more fish over 9lb than any of the lads at the time.

Fishing is seldom fair, but if you are determined enough, your day will come. So it was rather shame-faced that I ventured round to the 'Beach' the next morning, to assist with the photos of the biggest tench I have ever seen on the bank. I needn't have worried: everyone was great, and the fish was simply awesome!

A few days later the session came to an end. The highlight for me was a personal best perch of 3lb 11oz, though I struggled to appreciate it fully, having set eyes upon the two massive tench. Larry had a personal best tench of 9lb ½oz and was well pleased, and all of the newly formed 'Real Tench Fishers' except Warren caught (his time was yet to come). Because he was so desperate to catch a tench, I accompanied him to Larkfield 2 for a two-day session, where I bagged a few tench including a male of 7lb 7oz; but unfortunately for Warren, only a 5lb bream saved him from a dry net.

I returned to Ferris a few days later for a five-day session, but the fish weren't having it and I only managed a 5lb 4oz male. During the session Jackie Davis popped down with news that he had caught a tench of 10lb 5oz on a boilie whilst targeting carp at Wraysbury 1; he had also taken an 8lb-plus male, his third from the venue.

Bored with the lack of action and fuelled with the notion that there was still a chance of a 'double', Rory and I decided on a session on the Railway Lake. It was a hot Thursday afternoon when I arrived at the pit; there were a few anglers present, but the 'High Bank' swim on the causeway was free, so I set up there, and Rory was to join me at lunchtime the following day. I selected three clean gravelly areas to fish using the dinghy and marker floats. The view was unbelievable: I could see the bottom 16ft beneath me with the face mask. I baited all three areas with twenty balls of groundbait laced with hemp, wheat and

casters, but only managed to get the rods out by 10pm, due to the endless tea making and socializing. Then at 10.30pm the right rod ripped off, only to be weeded on the strike. Eventually I wound back my rig, but it was too dark to see my marker float for a re-cast, so I dropped it off with the dinghy.

With the earlier excitement and the droves of mosquitoes constantly buzzing around my ears, it was 2.30am before I got back to sleep; then I'm back up at 4.40am, just before the right rod does exactly the same as the previous night.

Standing there feeling gutted, I notice that my left marker float has disappeared: the '– carp' must have towed it off. I waited until 6am, then jumped in the dinghy and finally found it down the side of a small hump it had been resting on. I re-cast the rods, and almost immediately had a drop-back on the right rod. This resulted in no contact, but when I reeled in, the hook-length was gone just below the knot.

I tied a new hook-length and re-cast the rod, then settled down to some breakfast before it got too hot. Thankfully a cool northern wind picked up about 7am, making it at least bearable to sit on the exposed banks, and when the right rod roared into life for the fourth time, I made it count with a tench of 7lb 13oz that had taken the maggots. Thus re-inspired, I kept re-casting my three feeders, although the ever-strengthening crosswind was making it increasingly difficult. At 9.30am I missed a drop-back on the middle rod; cursing my luck, three casts later I was back in position.

I was just rolling a smoke when the middle one noted, and everything went everywhere, because suddenly I was playing a powerful fish. Heavy thumps pulsated down the rod as the fish came bankwards, then all went solid! Gently I tried to pump the fish out of the weedbed, but to no avail, and giving it slack line gained no result, either. Then one of the young lads who fish there turned up and offered to handline it from the dinghy.

After putting on my life jacket, he followed my line until he was over the fish, then with just the lightest of pulls he lifted the tench clear of the weedbed and I was playing it again. The fight was now unspectacular, as a large piece of weed was accompanying the tench bankwards, but the loud shouts of 'it's a massive tench!' did little to calm my nerves.

Eventually I netted her, just as two of the carp lads appeared ('Mad Steve' and 'Lowey'), and as soon as I saw her I knew my ambition had been achieved. Steve weighed her for me, I was in pieces, then he finished me off when the weight was given at 11lb 6oz. Everyone went mad: it was a venue record, and me, I was numb. For three years I had chased a goal, at the expense of all else, and now I had surpassed it by all expectations. I felt lost, with nowhere to go; that next run could be the personal best feeling, now at ridiculous odds. All the same, it was weeks before the smile left my face and the euphoria subsided a little.

I sacked her up so Rory could see her and take the photos, then tried to re-cast all the rods. The wind was now too strong to get the middle rod in place, so I rowed out, taking some groundbait with me. Having dropped the bait at the edge of the clear patch, I dropped my feeder over the edge, only to watch the wind drag it across the swim and into the weed. I rowed back, refilled the feeder, then made my way back to the spot – and as I looked over the side of the dinghy I saw what was surely another 10lb-plus tench eating my bait! It spooked when I got too close, and cursing my luck I lowered the feeder halfway to the bottom before letting go, only to see it towed out of the swim into the weed again!

When I returned for the third time a male of about 6lb was eating my bait, before moving off. This time I lowered my rig right on to the spot before returning to the bank. I had barely put the bobbin on when it tore off, and shortly afterwards I landed a 5lb 14oz male. Having never realized the effects of underflow and tension on the line, now rigs are always lowered fully on to the lake bed. Another lesson learnt at the expense of a good fish.

Rory came down and we caught a handful of fish over the next few sessions, including the big one two weeks later, down to an incredible 8lb 12oz. And that was it for 1995, as the summer was spent chasing other species.

I didn't venture back on to the Railway Lake until 3 July 1996, having been busy chasing doubles at three other venues, unsuccessfully. Again I chose the 'High Bank' swim, baiting the usual three areas, although the close in hump on the left was covered with silkweed.

Five runs the first day produced three tench, the best a 7lb 15oz male, and two hook pulls, one to a carp. The next day was better, with seven runs giving me five tench, topped off with the big one at 11lb 1oz, which started off the action on the weedy hump. The third day was quiet, with just a small tench and a bream, then it went mad on the last day, giving me eight tench and a bream by 1pm, when I ran out of bait; this was the biggest tench, a new fish of 10lb 2oz.

Again a couple more trips resulted in numerous fish, including a couple more 7lb-plus males, before my fishing took me elsewhere for the season.

On 12 June 1997, Chris and myself were camped in on the Railway Lake awaiting the off. I was back in the 'High Bank' swim, with Chris fifty yards past me in the 'Bridge'. The fridge had broken down in my local 'Apollo angling', and they had kindly let me have a bin liner full of casters. Much to the envy of the carp anglers, these were deposited into our swims, in an effort to clear some of our heavily weeded spots.

With Jim and Larry still fishing behind me on Larkfield, a good laugh was had awaiting the 16th. Eventually the time to cast out came, and almost unbelievably, at 6am on the first morning, I had the big one again at 11lb 4oz.

The action throughout the session was sparse, with myself netting seven other tench to 9lb 5oz, and a previously un-caught 18lb 7oz common. Chris caught roughly the same amount, topping off with an 8lb 13oz female and an enormous male of 8lb 11oz, possibly the biggest caught at the time.

A couple more trips with Jim Cheverall were almost fruitless, as the tench patrolled the margins, more interested in spawning. Sadly that's where my time at the Rail-way Lake ended, although I knew it con-tained other, possibly bigger tench; but I felt my name wasn't on them. It was time to leave the big girl in peace, but never forgotten, along with the magic of Johnsons.

WRAYSBURY 1

I first ventured on to Wraysbury 1 early in the spring of 1996. Although I had enjoyed some good fishing the previous spring on Larkfield 2, I wanted a water nearer to home, as roadworks on the M25 had proved a nightmare. I was to accompany an old fishing partner, Jackie Davis, who had already spent two seasons on there after its tench and carp, with a mutual friend Dave Smithers. They had caught a few tench on float tactics and feeder fish-ing, the best two both 9lb plus, and Jackie had also taken one of 10lb 5oz on a boilie whilst carp fishing.

A couple of walks round the pit and the limited success of Jackie and Dave did little to encourage any of the other lads to give it a go, especially with Larkfield guaranteeing action and quality. I liked the place, daunting as it was, and quickly secured a permit.

On 21 April Jackie and I dragged our tackle the three-quarters of a mile round to the 'Finger Bays', where he had caught a few tench the previous season. I didn't fancy the swim I was recommended: it was deep and weedy other than the marginal shelf, and I wanted to feeder fish. The pre-vious spring had revealed the importance of fishing the shallower bars, so I chose a swim with a small island halfway across the bay. The right side of the island shelved down slowly for a few yards and felt nice and gravelly, and I thought this could be a good spot to start on.

On further inspection with the plumbing rod, I found another gravel patch near the far bank margin under an overhanging dead tree. I baited each area with twenty balls of groundbait laced with hemp, wheat and casters, hoping a shoal of tench would pass through during my three-day trip.

The first night and day passed unevent-fully for both of us, with the weather turn-ing cold, wet and windy; no sign of any fish movement was evident, and to be truthful, a bit of pike fishing looked a better bet.

I put another dozen balls of groundbait on each spot for the second night, always liking something fresh in the swim. The evening was cold, and by 11pm I had retired to my bivvy, hoping the sun would reappear in the morning.

At 7.30am the far bank rod chugged into life, and after a spirited fight a long, lean tench lay in my net. Knowing it was over 8lb, I quickly weighed her, and was well pleased to see her register 9lb 2oz. She had succumbed to the pop-up maggot. What a welcome to Wraysbury! By midday I had added a 7lb 6oz bream and a 5lb 12oz male tench, both to the same rod, before I had to get home for my son David's party for his sixth birthday.

I was back at 8pm, rods out by five past, followed by ten balls of groundbait on each spot. I was just rolling another ten balls for the going spot when that rod roared off again as a tench of 7lb 5oz opted for the pop-up maggots. I wound in the other rod and popped the maggots up on that one as well, and unbelievably, ten minutes later a 10lb mirror carp had taken them.

Jackie was having no joy on his bomb and caster approach, so he borrowed a couple of feeders and tried to save himself from a blank. The night was quiet, and when I wound in my far bank rod, it had been weeded and the leeches had destroyed my hookbaits.

At 7.45am I pulled out of what felt like a tench on the island rod, but was only briefly connected to it. Then later at 9.10am I had one of 5lb 12oz from the far bank swim, followed by another of 5lb 14oz a couple of hours later, again on the same rod, and both to casters. Finally I pulled out of another tench on this rod on the popped-up maggot, before packing up in the mid-afternoon.

It had certainly been an entertaining first visit, and I was looking forward to returning, but I had arranged a few days at Larkfield with Chris Sullivan and Rory Adair, starting the next day. The trip accomplished, Chris succumbed to the lure of Wraysbury, with Rory following soon after.

The next trip to Wraysbury, a short twenty-four-hour session, resulted in a blank, after struggling to find any clear areas to fish. I had fished next to Jackie on the 'Douglas Point', where he had managed a couple of tench from a large shallow plateau; he had now taken up residence in the swim for the next month.

I returned a few days later to the same swim, this time armed with a dinghy, and Chris joined us for his maiden trip. A couple of hours with the dinghy and face mask revealed two gravel patches that took my fancy, one at ninety yards, and the other at about twenty yards out. Chris dropped into the right and fished near a dead tree in the bay, leaving the entire area well covered. During my absence Jackie had been landing a steady run of tench to nearly 9lb, and it came to light that he was in the top swim.

Chris landed a six-pounder within an hour of setting up, while I managed a similar-sized male during the afternoon. The night was quiet, and the following day gave me three 5lb-plus males all to the near-in spot, while Chris and Jackie managed a couple each.

The next day there was no action anywhere, and Chris departed in the early afternoon, leaving me to spend one more night. Again it was cold and frosty, and I was surprised when a persistent drop-back on the long-range rod resulted in a bream of 14lb ¼oz: what a bonus – a personal best and lake record all in one!

A couple more trips with Chris produced a few more moderate tench from a new area, while Jackie was still getting a few on the point, including a couple over 9lb and an 8lb 2oz male.

On my next visit the 'Root Nightmare' swim in the Douglas Lane car park was vacant, so I jumped in there. By the time I had found three clear spots and got my rods and bait out, it was 4pm, and everyone had used up my water, as I made endless cups of tea for them en route to their swims!

At 6.10pm a 6lb 9oz tench picked up the casters on my middle rod sixty yards out, then all remained quiet until a tiddler of 4lb arrived at first light.

The morning passed uneventfully, but the afternoon was hectic with myself landing another ten tench, the best going 9lb 2oz; Jackie popped round, having also had a good day, taking eight tench to 9lb 11oz. Things were definitely livening up, and the following morning I managed another two tench, plus a couple of 8lb bream before packing up.

The next trip saw Chris and myself on the North Lake, close to where Phil Gooriah's record had been taken. We both landed several tench, with a few eight-pounders amongst them; then, come 16 June, everyone congregated on Ferris in the hope of a 12lb-plus monster.

A few days later Chris and I were back at Wraysbury in the Dredger Bay, and again were amongst the fish, landing several tench to almost 9lb. By now, the carp lads were beginning to wonder where all the tench were coming from, as they seldom caught more than four or five a season between them.

Desperate for a 'double', the next month was spent between Johnsons Railway Lake and Ferris Meadow, and by the time I returned to Wraysbury it was late July and the weed was horrendous. A thick algal bloom made spotting clear patches impossible, and with only limited knowledge of the pit and a couple of blanks under my belt, I decided Wraysbury would have to keep to next spring, at least as far as the tench were concerned.

On 11 April 1997, Chris and myself started our tench season back in the 'Fingerbays'; I fished my island swim, with Chris seventy yards up, where two of the bays joined. Chris enjoyed the best of the action, taking ten tench in a day, the best a 7lb 4½oz male, whilst I only managed three tench; the best of these, however, was a new personal best male of 8lb 2oz. A twenty-four-hour blank followed in the same swim a few days later, before I ventured into a new area of the Pit called 'No Carp Bay' for a three-day session. This started slowly, with nothing until after dark on the second night, when a small tench picked up a bunch of maggots. A 7lb 15oz specimen followed at lunchtime, whilst in the evening I landed an 8lb 12oz female and a new personal best male of 8lb 5oz.

A couple of short sessions produced a tench or two, but nothing of note; but at the same time Larkfield 2 was fishing its head off, and Jim was back on the fishing minus a Wraysbury ticket, so the bulk of my time was being spent in Kent. It was near the end of May, when a two-day session in the 'Root Nightmare' produced five tench to 9lb 1oz and a 15lb carp; but the chances of a 'double' looked better elsewhere, and again the Wraysbury tench fishing was over for another season.

The 1998 season saw a change in the rules, with no fishing until 1 June; I had spent the spring bagging up on two other pits, and never made it to Wraysbury until the 7 June when a twenty-four-hour session in the 'Root Nightmare' gave me a 9lb 13oz beast early in the morning.

A trip to the 'Grassy Slope' on the North Lake with Chris and Rory gave me another ten tench to 9lb 2oz, including an 8lb 1oz male, with both Chris and Rory also taking 9lb-plus specimens. This year the tench were carrying later than on my other venues, so Rory and I carried on in search of a 'double'.

Three days later I joined Rory on the 'Douglas Point', and on arrival found he had taken several fish from the shallow plateau, topped by giants of 9lb 1oz, 9lb 12oz and 10lb 1½oz. The weather was hot, so I didn't fancy the featureless swim next to him, and opted to fish a couple of humps in the back bay.

During the night my right rod kept knocking and bleeping, leaving me hovering over it waiting for a run. It wasn't until it was fully light that it finally roared off, and after an anxious few moments near some marginal bushes, I hauled a large tench into the safety of my net. At 10lb 3oz it was my first Wraysbury 'double', a fish I had wanted for some time; and less than an hour later the other rod produced another of 9lb 13oz. And I couldn't believe it when the next day delivered me a further two lumps of 9lb 2oz and 9lb 13oz, along with a few lesser specimens. Wraysbury had come on form with a vengeance – but sadly the tench soon spawned.

A couple more half-hearted tench/eel sessions produced 8lb 9oz and 9lb 2oz specimens, before I accepted that the best of the fishing had passed, and concentrated on the eels.

By the following season Jim Cheverall was accompanying me on most trips, and was eager for a taste of the Wraysbury tench fishing. I couldn't get down there until 3 June due to work, but thankfully when we arrived for a marathon thirteen-day session the 'Douglas Point' was available. Like two men possessed, we hurried round there with our tackle to secure the two swims on the end of the point, then spent all day getting sorted.

By the time the rods were all out it was 8pm and we were both starving; as the barbecue gently smoked beside us we sat watching the pit, anticipating our fortunes. I was in the left swim facing the large plateau for the first time; it was as weedy as ever, but with the boat well fishable, I knew it wouldn't be long before the tench made an appearance.

A one-noter dragged me from my bed chair at 1.15am, and at 7lb 6oz my first Wraysbury tench of the season was soon on the bank. Others of 7lb 7oz and 8lb 9oz joined it in the next couple of hours, then it went dead until early next morning when three runs produced fish of 5lb 5oz, a 6lb 4oz male and a hook pull.

Jim's swim remained quiet, but he said he was confident of getting some action, and kept plodding away at it. The next morning brought me two more males of 7lb and 6lb 4oz by 8am, before the unbearable heat put an end to any feeding activity for the day.

I asked Jim if he wanted to share my swim in the shallower water, but he assured me he was happy to stay put. The following morning was quiet with my only run coming at 11.25am from a plump tench of 8lb 7oz.

With the midday sun high in the sky I sat sheltering under some trees near my bivvy, when I heard a strange sound coming from next door: it was one of Jim's buzzers. As I came round my camp I could see he was bent into a fish, and by the way his rod kept stabbing I guessed it was a male tench. A couple of minutes later Jim was on the score sheet with a personal best male of 6lb 15oz, and I hoped his luck had changed.

At about 3pm he was in again, and another tench; this one, weighing 7lb 5oz, was soon hanging on the Avons. We both re-baited our spots in the early evening, then after dinner sat watching the pit, hoping to see some activity over the bait.

Nothing was showing, and we were both surprised when one of Jim's rods screamed off, and he bent into what was obviously a better fish. The tench took line heading out into the pit before turning round and kiting into the large tree in the water that separated our swims. We could hear it splashing out of sight behind some branches, so I grabbed a landing net and jumped into the dinghy.

As I approached the tree I could see a large tench sitting six inches below the surface under a couple of thick branches; I relayed the information to Jim, and told him to get ready to pay out line, once I had hopefully netted it. I eased the dinghy towards the tench trying not to spook it, but as I tried to slide the net under it, the net was pushing the dinghy outwards. On the third attempt I managed to grab hold of a branch and then net the tench one-handed – and thankfully it behaved. I bit through the line above Jim's rig, then rowed the tench back to the shore.

We soon had her on the scales, and at 9lb 4oz it was Jim's second biggest; at last things were going his way, and I got my turn behind the camera for a change. We sat and enjoyed his triumph, eventually getting to bed around 11pm, tired from getting up early and the endless heat.

The next thing I knew it was the early hours and Jim's buzzer woke me; I got round there just in time to slip the net under another fat tench. This time the scales registered 9lb 7oz, and after sacking her in the deep margin, I shook Jim's hand and went back to bed. Jim remained awake, the two big tench heavily on his mind as he anticipated further action.

At 5.45am I awoke to Jim shaking me: he had just landed a lump of 10lb 3oz and was holding it in the weigh sling. I jumped up and we both shared its beauty; I knew how he must have felt, I could still

June 1999: Jim with 'John Holmes' at 8lb 12oz.

remember my own joy at catching my first 'double'. We popped her in the sack next to her comrades, while we calmed down and waited for the sun to rise a little higher, for the photos.

The day progressed slowly, with the only run producing an 8lb 1oz male to myself mid-morning. Jim was buzzing all day, I had never seen him work his feeders so hard. I hoped his sport would continue. A few of the carp lads dropped in that evening to celebrate Jim's success, and a good time was had by all. Eventually everyone retired to their own swims or homes, leaving Jim and I to clean up the debris.

During the night Jim popped round to inform me he had taken an 8lb 12oz male, but tiredness was upon me, and apparently all I said was 'Are you sure?', then went back to sleep. I was awoken by a 7lb 10oz tench at 6.20am on my left rod; Jim was sleeping, and I must have been half way through a cup of coffee when Jim's big male crossed my mind. Still unsure if I had dreamt it, I wandered round to his swim, and sure enough, something was in the sack. I put the kettle on; he would have to get up, I wanted to know for sure.

As the kettle boiled I dragged him from his grave, and he confirmed he had indeed caught an 8lb 12oz male. He didn't seem to realize the significance, but after I explained he had just beaten Chris Sullivan's group record by an ounce, I saw that big old grin reappear on his face.

We measured the specimen before the photos at 22½in long, with a girth of 18½in: what a beast! He bore a few scars here and there from where he had been entertaining the ladies on the spawning grounds, so we named him 'John Holmes' after the famous porn star.

Sadly Jim's action had come to an end, and the next seven days produced only a 6lb 12oz male for him; but he was more than happy with what he had already caught, and contented himself soaking up the atmosphere.

As Jim's swim died, my swim re-awoke on a slow but steady basis. Over the next six days I landed another twelve tench, and lost a few on hook pulls due to weed. I had some good fish: best females were 9lb 1½oz, 9lb 3oz and 9lb 14oz, and I also managed 'John Holmes' at 8lb 9oz, a new personal best male.

As we sat there on the final evening, I wondered if I would get my 'double'; I had been close, and Jim knew how much I needed to catch one. We sat up late, and at 12.15am my left rod roared off: unbelievably it was 'John Holmes' again, down a bit more in weight at 8lb 5oz. We laughed as we put him back in the margin, before retiring to bed.

I was awoken at 5.30am by a one-noter on my left rod; as I bent into it a good tench took line as it powered off. Then it weeded me, but I got it moving again, and Jim was beside me, waiting with the net as I brought her bankwards. Steadily she came, heavy thumps pulsating down the rod – and then she was gone! The hook had pulled out, I was sunk, I was sure it was a good fish.

Jim tried to console me, as I resisted the urge to throw my rod down in frustration. Time was against me to catch the desired one; days had turned into hours, and soon it would be time to leave.

I quickly changed the hook, although it appeared all right, and cast my feeder back on to the spot. Jim put the kettle on, and I went about re-casting my other rods; I was just winding in the second one when the left rod roared into action again.

Another good tench powered outwards into the pit, and I held the rod high, trying to keep it above the weed. My legs were shaking as slowly I turned her and brought her towards the bank, expecting the hook to pull at any moment. Finally she was in sight, and as she tried to swing across the swim, Jim netted her under the water and pulled her to safety.

As we unhooked her, we both knew the score: and sure enough, the Avons thumped down to 10lb 11oz, and we both went crazy! What a tench: 25in long with a girth of 19¼in, and it easily had the potential to be at least a pound heavier. Photos were taken, and she was returned to the marginal depths from where she had come.

The morning passed uneventfully, and it was two very satisfied anglers who carried their tackle back to the car park.

We returned a week later for a two-day session, but the tench were busy spawning throughout. Then just as we were due back for a week, the water was closed to protect its stock from SVC. By the time it had reopened it was time for some eel fishing, although a couple of days feedering in late September did give me six tench over 8lb, and four upper-double stockies.

During the spring of 2000, Wraysbury was given SSSI status, forcing it to remain closed until 16 June. With another hot spring gone by, I wondered if the tench were still carrying much spawn, as I set up alone on the 'Douglas Point' on 15 June.

The fish were reasonably cooperative with me landing twenty-three tench and a pike over my nine-day session. Sadly any recognizable tench were all down in weight by about a pound, with my best tench going 9lb 2oz, backed up by a few upper eight-pounders.

This was my last session on Wraysbury for tench, as pastures new and old called me away. I still contemplate returning, because it's a water you can become totally absorbed with: who knows what leviathans lie beneath its depths, and each time your buzzer sounds, anything could be on the end.

FERRIS MEADOW, 1998 SEASON

With Wraysbury 1 not open until 1 May to give the carp a rest, and Larkfield only producing two 9lb-plus tench so far, out of over 200, the prospects of getting the season's first 'double' under my belt were looking grim. Then in mid-May, news reached me that Ferris Meadow was between tenancies and was available to fish on a 'guesting' basis.

Having always felt that the place owed me a 'double', I was soon baiting an area known as the 'Beach' ready for a two-day session. Rory and Jackie were on the opposite bank, with Rory already having landed a few good tench.

I pulled up by the hole in the fence around 1am, quickly poked my tackle through, then parked the car up the road out of sight. Like a man possessed I hurried to my swim and had three feeders in position by 2am; the bivvy would keep till after it got light.

As I sat there wondering what the morning would bring, a small eel took a liking to a bunch of casters seventy yards out, near the end of the island. As it slithered off into the darkness I hoped it would be the last of the night. I had forgotten about all the small eels at Ferris, having been spoiled by a couple of seasons on waters only containing a few large ones.

Dawn came and went, with Rory landing 8lb 10oz and 9lb 7oz specimens just after first light. It was 7am by the time my left rod roared off, as a small tench of 4lb 13oz picked up the casters on a little hump halfway to the island. At least I was on the score sheet.

As the sun climbed higher we knew it was going to be a scorcher of a day; occasional fish rolled here and there on the mirror-like surface, and I knew they were going to be having it. It was nearly 9am: I had just finished sorting my camp out, trying to hide from the sun, when my right rod, sixty yards out in nine foot of open water, roared into life. After a lively battle in the margins a short plump female of 6lb 1oz was being returned, showering me with a couple of heavy slaps of her tail as she departed.

At about 10am, Rory shouted across and I went round to help photo a beast of 10lb 11oz for him; he was on a 'roll', and I knew he would have some more. I rushed back to my swim and had only just sat down after casting my rods, when the one near the island ripped off – and instantly I knew it was a better fish, the slow heavy plodding giving the game away. Eventually she succumbed to the waiting net, and as I lay her on the mat and saw her girth I thought I may have a 'double'; however, as I drew back the mesh I could see she was very short. On the scales she went a very respectable 9lb 5oz, and Rory popped round and took the photos.

As the day got hotter I dozed in my chair under the umbrella, not wanting to stray from my rods. In the early afternoon I had another tench of 7lb 9oz from near the island on a bunch of maple cream-flavoured maggots; and that was the last of the action for the day.

I slept well that night, not rising until 9am; with the sun hidden behind the clouds, it was a lot more pleasant. After a quick brew I re-cast all the rods and settled down on my chair, angry at myself for not getting up early. I always like to watch the water at dawn and re-cast with fresh baits; sometimes I introduce a few balls of plain brown crumb just to colour the water and highlight my spots.

Every twenty minutes or so, I re-cast the rods, hoping to induce some action – and as always, just as I started cooking some late breakfast around midday, the open-water rod one-noted. A powerful fish immediately took a couple of yards of line, before plodding deep, then kiting to my right. I gained as much line as I could standing wader deep in the margin, trying to stop it reaching the sanctuary of the branches hanging into the margins to my right. A couple of yards short of possible tragedy it stopped and I managed to pump it straight to the net.

Immediately I could see it was a big fish, and as I unhooked her, a tell-tale black mark on her cheek told me it was Rory's 12lb-plus from 1995. I hung her on the Avons, not quite knowing what to expect, and as they settled on 10lb 14½oz, I shouted across. I sacked her in a deep margin nearby and shortly afterwards three cameras captured the moment forever, my first Ferris 'double'.

That evening a lake record 7lb 3oz male graced my net, but unfortunately my head was still too full of the earlier giant to fully appreciate the moment.

I was woken up early at 3.30am by an 8lb 14oz bream, so decided to stay up and work the feeders hard for the day, until I left. At about 9.30am I had a tench of 7lb 9oz, then in the early afternoon I lost a similar-sized one, when the hook fell out just short of the net. As I packed away I was itching to get back.

I decided to start fishing nights between shifts at work, which meant I had to leave the pit by 6am, so I opted for a shallow corner area known as 'The Shed', (on a shed full) that was a good night swim.

The first visit produced a 9lb bream, and I was back at 6.30pm the following evening with Chris Sullivan for another try.

I positioned two feeders thirty yards out in a seven-foot deep gulley, and a third on a small sandy patch to my right. Forty balls of groundbait went into the gulley, with just a dozen on the other spot, before I settled down to do battle with the mosquitoes.

At 11.30pm, just as I was having a tidy up before bed, a 10lb 4oz bream picked up a couple of 10mm boilies in the gulley. Then all was quiet until 3.30am when I bumped another bream on the same rod.

The alarm clock woke me at 5am. Feeling as if I had just shut my eyes, I dragged myself from the warmth of my sleeping bag, woke Chris, and put the kettle on. The swim looked lifeless as I started to pack away, but I would be back in the Beach tonight with a day off work to follow.

With everything packed but the rods, we were just about to photo my bream when one of the gulley rods screamed off and I was bent into what was obviously not another bream. A few minutes later we were admiring a massive tench on the mat; as I rolled her over for a better look I saw the distinctive black mark on the chin and exclaimed to Chris, 'It's black spot again!'.

Knowing I had just caught her took the edge off the moment a little, but at 10lb 12½oz it was still a very happy angler heading to work that morning.

I did a few more sessions at Ferris before the owner apprehended some people and the fishing had to stop. I had a few more tench to 8lb 11oz, but the highlight was a lake record bream of 13lb 14oz, followed a few days later by a brace of bream at 13lb 10oz and 13lb 9oz. Rory also managed a few more good fish topped off by a brace of tench at 10lb 9oz and 10lb 4oz.

SHEEPWALK

With Wraysbury 1 being afforded SSSI status the spring fishing came to an end, and with Ferris Meadow now being controlled by a certain unsavoury character, a new venue was needed for the spring of 2000.

A local pit of around 30 acres had caught my eye a few times over the years, but previous reconnaissance trips to the water had gone unrewarded. The few tench I had seen only appeared to be in the 4lb–5lb bracket, and with little sign of other anglers being present, information was hard to come by.

With my fiancé, Lesley, expecting a child at the end of May, I needed to fish locally as my time would be limited. The mystery of the 'Sheepwalk' called to me, and I took up the challenge.

By mid-April I had spent a fair bit of time walking round and plumbing the pit, the bulk of which I had found to be in excess of 20ft deep. In all but a few swims on the north bank, where two large islands lay and a shallower channel ran between them and the bank, the marginal shelf dropped straight to 16ft, deepening as it progressed outwards. With so much deep water and the apparent lack of bars, I decided to target the marginal shelf and the shallow north bank where the water would warm up quickest.

I baited four margin spots with hemp and casters a couple of times, then fished two mornings on the float, roving between them; but to no avail. The only action came from an eel of about 1½lb that momentarily made my heart race. There was no sign of any fish activity on these trips, so I decided I would bait the island margin in the north-east corner, and take my son David for a couple of days the forthcoming weekend, to give his mum some peace.

We arrived in the late afternoon, and after setting up home I assembled three feeder rods. David's was a simple running block-end fished with maggots for the eels, while I fished 2oz open-end feeders with a variety of baits for tench. My left rod was cast 5yd from the island margin into 15ft of water at the bottom of the slope, with the right rod 20yd out into 18ft of water nearer the corner. Both areas were baited with thirty balls of groundbait laced with hemp, wheat and casters, and left until dusk to settle.

As day became night a steady run of eels up to 1½lb came to David's rod, before he retired to bed. I had a couple myself, and a couple of short drop-backs that may have been liners.

The day passed uneventfully, other than meeting a carp angler named Stuart, who suggested an area near the north-west corner where he had caught a few tench up to 7lb the previous season. I topped up both my areas with another twenty balls of bait each, before settling down to another evening's eel bashing.

It was still cold at night, and thankfully we only managed two each before 11pm, when I bent into something heavy on the rod near the island. I couldn't believe it when seconds later what felt like a good bream fell off. Wondering whether my popped-up maggots had foul-hooked it, I decided to change to bread, hoping there might be some more good ones out there.

I had another small eel on my right rod – and that was fishing bread as well – and then retired at about 1am. I was awoken by a steady drop-back on the island rod at about 3.30am, and was quickly bent into something a bit too powerful to be a bream. After a spirited battle in the deep, weed-free water, I drew a good tench over the net and could immediately see in the torchlight she was very long. David came out because of all the disturbance, and we soon had her weighed at 9lb 2oz. I was well pleased; what a welcome to the new water. The tench had enormous potential at 25in long with a girth of 17½in, and I knew the fish could easily surpass 11lb.

Although I stayed up and worked the feeders, no more action was forthcoming

so we packed up at lunchtime. Before we left I baited two areas in the swim Stuart had suggested, although looking at the submerged oil drum, lumps of metal, car tyres and fallen trees in the water I knew the fishing would be difficult – in fact I christened the swim 'The Scrapyard'.

The following morning I returned at first light, and after seeing a couple of tench roll over my bait near the island, I sat expectantly. At 6.15am a liner on that rod had me leaping from the chair, then all remained quiet until 10.10am when I had a tench of 7lb 15oz from the near-in spot. The fish had taken a maggot and caster cocktail that had been pugged into the feeder, as the sandy hump it was fishing on was coated in silkweed.

Well pleased with the tench, I carried on re-casting both rods every twenty minutes or so, until at 12.30pm the island rod ripped off and another tench of 7lb 5oz was in the net, having taken a fancy to my popped-up maggot.

I had to leave shortly afterwards as I was due at work that night and needed some sleep. Before I left I put thirty balls of bait on each spot to start building the swim, and the following night I baited again on my way to work, being careful not to leave any evidence.

The following morning straight from work I fished between 8.30am until 12.30pm, missing the only run at 8.45am on the near-in spot. I baited before I left, and again the following night on the way to work.

The following morning it went mad between 8.55am and 11.30am: I had nine runs resulting in seven tench between 5lb 9oz and 7lb 14oz, mainly to the island rod. I only managed one tench on the near-in rod, although my rod top was regularly knocking as fish hit the line; even the popped-up maggots couldn't buy a run

157

there. I reluctantly packed up at 12.40pm as I was due back at work at 4.30pm for a fifteen-hour shift.

I continued to bait the swim most nights, but my next after-work visit resulted in just one tench of 7lb 3oz in cold, wet conditions. I baited again that night on the way to work, knowing it would be my last shift for twelve nights, as I was due some holiday and also had an early finish in the morning.

I was back in the 'Scrapyard' swim fishing by 6am the following morning, looking forward to two full days and a night's fishing. The weather was mild and overcast with the occasional sunny spell, and at 7.40am a 5½lb male opened the proceedings on the island rod; this was quickly followed by a liner, then pulling out of a tench on the same rod.

A carp angler called Graham who was fishing the swim behind me on a different pit, came over for a chat; as we talked the island rod roared into life again, and after a brief but hectic battle, a personal best common carp of 27lb 10oz lay on the mat. It was one of the best-looking carp I had ever seen, and apparently the new lake record for commons.

The swim went quiet, but I was content to sit, occasionally re-casting my feeders hoping to get a response from something. At 11.55am the island rod roared off again and I suspected I was attached to another carp, but as it came closer in the shallow water I could see it was a large tench. Suddenly it powered through a half-sunken tree in the left margin, and all went solid. Distraught I slackened the line, put the bait runner on, and waited. After a minute or two the line slowly picked up, and then the bait runner clicked into life; I let it take maybe three or four yards before bending back into it; thankfully the line pulled clear of the branches, and I netted it without further problem.

At 9lb 12oz I was absolutely delighted. The pit was turning into a goldmine – but best of all, the mystery remained, in that every time the buzzer went off, anything could be on the end. Another five tench up to 6lb 6oz brought me back to earth during the afternoon, before the eels forced a change of bait to bread by midnight.

Although many fish were rolling over the island swim during the night, only one small tench picked up the bread before I got up at 5.30am and changed back to maggots and casters. Throughout the day I had a steady run of action, accounting for twelve tench up to 7lb 3oz, mainly on the island rod; but the near-in patch was also starting to produce as the tench cleared the silkweed.

Whilst packing everything away, a young carp angler informed me he had caught a 9lb 10oz tench a few days earlier and had seen a couple of other large tench in an area in the south-west corner; so next trip I decided to give it a try. The night and morning went by without a bite, and by lunchtime I was back in the 'Scrapyard'.

I baited my two spots as usual, and fished bread and mini boilies throughout the night to no avail. Dragging myself from my pit at first light revealed a few tench rolling over the inside rod, so I quickly rebaited my rods with maggots and casters and awaited the action. It started at 5.50am with a 7lb 2oz tench on the inside rod, and continued until 2.20pm, by which time I had amassed nine tench to 9lb 7oz, two 6lb-plus bream, and a 16lb 9oz common carp. This time the tench were from a different shoal, with only two fish going under 7lb: it made for quite a day's fishing.

For the next two weeks I was kept busy with visits to the hospital and work, but I still managed a few short sessions, resulting in a dozen or so tench to 7½lb – and young David managed a couple as well! Finally on 29 May I had a young daughter

Kathryn (9lb plus, of course) and some more holiday to look forward to.

A couple of early morning sessions with young David gave mother and baby some peace, and then I had a chance of having two days to myself. By now I was starting to wonder if I would get my double-figure tench, as June was upon me and the weather had been pretty hot – and surely the tench would spawn soon.

It was mid-afternoon as I set up home in the 'Scrapyard', the weather warm with a gentle south-westerly breeze blowing down to me. Eager to get started, I baited both areas and had my baits in position by 4pm. I had a few mates popping down later to wet the baby's head, and I was looking forward to some company: it had been a lonely spring.

At about 5.30pm the action started, with a 6oz perch grabbing my maggot and caster cocktail on the near-in rod, followed soon after by a small tench on the island rod. Over the next forty minutes I took another tench on each rod, the best weighing 8lb 1oz, taken on casters near the island. Occasionally fish were rolling over both areas, and it looked to be a promising start to the session.

At about 7pm my mate Jim Cheverall arrived, and just as he put his bag down in the swim, my near-in rod roared into life. As I bent into it, the fish powered across the swim towards the channel on my left. Jim commented on the bend in my rod, suggesting what I already thought, that it was a good fish. I turned her, and then she came straight at me, trying to seek sanctuary in the weed and debris below her; but I pulled hard, and she surfaced five yards out, displaying her deep flank. We both knew she could go 10lb plus, which didn't help my nerve as she charged towards the semi-sunken branches in the margin. I hung on and gave her the butt, watching every inch of the battle in the clear water.

The hook held firm and she turned inches from possible disaster, before rolling beaten on the surface and allowing me to draw her to my waiting net.

As we laid her on the unhooking mat and removed the hook she looked every inch a double; and then I recognized a couple of marks on her flank, and realized it was the 9lb 7oz tench I had caught nearly three weeks earlier, which had dropped from 9lb 12oz in the five days prior to that. Rather uncertainly I lowered her on to the Avons; but I needn't have worried as the needle shot past the 10lb mark before settling at 10lb 7oz. I danced with jubilation: my quest had been achieved. I had taken a gamble on a new, unknown venue and it had given me a great reward: this tench would always be a very special 'double' to me.

A few phone calls later, and five of us admired her beauty as I held her for the photos; we then watched her swim back to her underwater world. No more action was forthcoming that evening, and I wound in the rods at 8.45pm for the double celebration drink. The tench would keep till the morning.

As the evening progressed only Jim and myself remained; we talked of the great tench the evening had produced, and of others that had gone before it on our travels. Wraysbury was calling us for the 16 June opening, its ever-mysterious waters always capable of producing something enormous; and Papercourt had given us a lot of good fish last July when fate had placed us there. Eventually in the early hours I crawled on to my bed chair and passed out, leaving Jim asleep on the path behind me looking somewhat like a 'down and out'.

It was gone 7am when he woke me shouting something about 'bubbles' and 'Jacuzzi'. Ten minutes later as I sat up I could see what he meant: my near-in patch

June 2000: the mystery of the Sheepwalk called, and gave me this beauty of 10lb 7oz.

was literally foaming – I had never seen anything like it, the surface above the whole of the baited area was bubbling profusely. Another ten minutes passed before two swim-feeders splashed into position and two buzzers beeped into life, as one very expectant angler settled down in his chair next to his rods.

The action started ten minutes later and carried on for two hours, during which time I landed eight of the nine tench I hooked, unfortunately losing one after it kited into some sunken branches. The tench ranged from 5lb 6oz to 7lb 13oz, with surprisingly only two fish coming from the near-in swim, although the rod top was knocking almost continuously.

I did a few more sessions on the Sheepwalk, but the best of the fishing had passed. The action slowed down considerably, with a few low eight-pounders being the better fish; even trying another couple of swims didn't produce anything. In fact I had had my fill; there was time to see what Wraysbury still had to offer – although it would take a very special tench to put a bigger smile on my face than my 'Scrapyard double'!

PAPERCOURT

Following my Sheepwalk campaign I did a nine-day session on Wraysbury 1's 'Douglas Point'. As mentioned in the Wraysbury chapter, many of the fish had spawned, and with the hot weather continuing, prospects of a 'double' didn't look good; so I thought I would spend the last two nights of my holiday at Papercourt, where hopefully I would bag a few tench without too much effort. Fate first sent me to Papercourt a year earlier, when Wraysbury 1 had been closed the day before I started a week's holiday, due to numerous carp deaths around the country. Jim Cheverall and myself had our tackle sorted and bait ordered for a week's tench fishing, so after a quick phone call to Ian Welch we decided to spend our week at Papercourt.

On that occasion friends Chris Sullivan and Warren Hammond had done a few days at the start of the season and had caught a few tench to 9lb 11oz, so we knew there were some reasonable fish present, but with nearly three weeks passed we had guessed the tench would be spawned out, and this was to be more of a pleasure session. The weather had been hot when we arrived, making the long walk to the suggested swims on the opposite bank look tedious, so we had settled into the nearest double swim to the right of the car park. A quick plumb round had revealed an almost steady seven feet all over, with plenty of

silkweed present, so we had decided to fish at varying ranges between ten and seventy yards, hoping to intercept any tench shoals moving through the area.

The usual swim-feeder and heavy groundbait approach was adopted, and as day turned to night on the first evening, the action had commenced. The fish had obviously never seen this approach before, as by the end of the week I had amassed forty-seven tench to 8lb 8oz (with twenty-six topping 7lb, including six over 8lb), three bream to 9lb 1oz, and twelve carp to 20lb 3oz. Jim had managed thirteen tench, one of which was 9lb 15oz, a tremendous fish, and five carp.

By the time we left we knew we would be returning another year, because except for Jim's largest fish, the others had all dropped their spawn – so the potential for this water was amazing.

This year on arrival I was surprised to find only three other cars in the car park, one being loaded ready to depart. A quick chat with the angler resulted in tales of doom and gloom, with apparently little being caught since the start. Not too disheartened, I wandered down to the swims we had fished the previous year, and on finding them empty, promptly set up in my usual side.

Using my normal all-or-nothing approach, I deposited 100 balls of groundbait containing hemp, wheat and four pints of casters on to each of the two areas I had fished the year before. Because of the tightness of the swim and the amount of action I was expecting, I opted to fish with only two rods in order to minimize the chances of crossed lines when playing fish.

With everything done, I settled down and put the kettle on. The evening was still warm, the only sign of life on the water being some mallards that were mopping up the dry bits from my baiting. When the buzzer on my right rod roared into life

July 1999: Jim Cheverall with a superb-looking Papercourt specimen of 9lb 15oz.

twenty minutes later I thought a rogue 'tufty' was to blame, but a steady thumping pulsated up the rod and soon a 6lb 10oz tench was being weighed.

All was quiet for a couple of hours, before another tench of 7lb 6oz fell to popped-up maggots on my other rod. Things were looking promising, but I managed to bump the next two tench during the night, before landing a small eel at 2.45am. As I re-cast I could make out fish rolling over the spot I had baited further out, so I decided to re-cast that rod as well. I had barely nodded back off when it was away, with a lively male of 6lb 14oz that seemed to take a dislike to the shallow margins and landing net.

I cast the rod back out and put the kettle on, since any chance of getting some sleep seemed futile, besides which it would be light within the hour. But the dawn chorus came and went, and even though I regularly re-cast both rods, the bobbins remained motionless, although occasionally dark backs broke the surface over both spots. By 6am I was hungry, but I had only just finished cooking breakfast when a steady drop-back on the rod further out indicated that the tench were in similar mood. After a brief but lively fight I was weighing a specimen of 8lb 9oz, which I quickly popped in a sack while I ate.

I had just returned it after a couple of quick snaps when the bait runner on the near-in rod went into overdrive as a tench of 8lb 5oz sought sanctuary in the middle of the pit. Then, unbelievably, as I netted it the other rod burst into life, so I rested the landing net against the rushes before playing the other tench safely to the second net (I always take two with me for exactly such a situation). At 7lb 1oz, this one was a bit smaller, but still a nice fish. This was turning into quite a session!

All was quiet for the next forty-five minutes, then the rod further out gave me three fish in the following forty minutes, at 9lb 6oz, 9lb 4oz and 8lb 7oz: I was going mad! Most of the fish were taking maggots popped up six inches off the bottom, obviously preferring not to dig through the silkweed for their dinner. Then after a biteless hour I guessed the fish had moved on, so I tidied my swim before firing another thirty balls of bait on to each spot. I dozed on my chair in the midday sun, more than happy with the day's sport, and with no idea that it had far from finished.

Between 2.30pm and 4.30pm four smaller tench came to my net, again all to the further rod. After dinner I put another fifty balls of groundbait on the distant rod, but only twenty on the other, as it had received little action. Then at about 8.30pm, after a long battle in the margins, the near-in spot came up trumps, with a

beauty of 9lb 1oz, followed an hour later by one of 8lb 2oz on the other rod. I could hardly believe the day's events – so much for the leisurely approach, this was tench fishing of the highest quality.

During the night a small eel, an 8lb bream and two 7lb-plus tench kept the far-out rod busy and me sleepless until 3am. I then slept like the dead until 10am when the sun forced me from my camp and it was time to leave. I knew I would be back.

After seven nights at work I was back in the same swim for a twenty-four-hour session. It was 3pm by the time I had performed the usual groundbait routine, though I only put out seventy balls on each spot as it was a short session. As dusk drew in, the near-in patch gave me two 7lb-plus tench ten minutes apart, and I braced myself for another sleepless night.

But it wasn't to be, and the alarm clock woke me at 4.30am. It had been a cool, clear night, and a fine layer of mist lay over the lake's surface: a perfect tench fisher's dawn was in the making. As I sipped at my coffee debating the ethics of crashing 3oz of swim-feeder into the perfect oily calm, I was disturbed by a one-noter on the near-in rod. After a spirited fight, a long black tench wallowed over the landing net; as I unhooked her I guessed she was 8lb plus, but I still couldn't believe it when she went 10lb 6oz on the Avons! I carefully reweighed her at the same weight, then had a good look at her: she had no gut on her, but was very thick across the back and sides, measuring 24in long with a girth of 19¼in. I sacked her up while I got my head round it; I was well chuffed, and got on the phone to persuade Jim Cheverall to get out of bed and come and take the photos.

Less than an hour passed before a pot-bellied tench of 8lb 13oz was in the neighbouring sack, and by the time Jim had arrived at 6.30am a couple of smaller ones had been returned. After the photos we watched them both swim off; side by side in the water the black one looked much bigger, although on the mat it looked the smaller. A couple more seven-pounders around lunchtime brought the session to an end, and one happy angler bounced back to the car park.

For whatever reason I didn't return for another eight days, only doing so after agreeing to do a feature for *Angling Times*. I visited my swim before work the night before and baited it up; I was finishing early in the morning and hoped it would still be vacant at 5.30am when I returned. I needn't have worried; only the same three cars were still in the car park when I returned with my tackle, the so-said poor quality of the angling having driven many away to pastures new.

I had both rods out by 6.30am, long before the camera crew was due to arrive, and hopeful of some early morning sport; but it never materialized. At about 10am, with the crew due in an hour, I decided to put another twenty balls of groundbait on each spot to colour up the water and hopefully attract some tench into the area.

At about 10.45am the crew of Dave Woodmansey and Mick Rouse approached, mugs in hand, and I informed them that it was not looking promising. It was a real scorcher of a day and the pit looked lifeless. We sat and chatted and went through a few rigs, when suddenly I had a drop-back on the further rod. After a good fight, I netted a tench of 8lb 11oz; this highly excited the lads, and it was followed fifteen minutes later by one of 7lb 8oz. They did what they needed to do, wished me well, and left me to my fishing.

As the afternoon passed I landed three more 7lb-plus tench, all on the further rod. Another angler settled into the swim next door, and we spent the evening chatting; by

9pm I was ready for bed, having been up for twenty-eight hours. The night was chilly and damp, and when the buzzer sounded at 2.20am on the near-in rod, I was reluctant to leave the warmth of my sleeping bag. Blurry-eyed, I bent into a powerful fish that immediately took fifteen yards of line off the clutch; it then kited to the left, going under my other rod and forcing me to pass my rod under as well. Eventually I got her under control and netted her, just as the angler next door came round to see what was causing all the commotion.

As I lay the net on the mat and peeled back the mesh I knew it was a 'double'; my hands were trembling as I removed the size 10 Super Specialist from the corner of its lip, the little polyball still attached. On the scales it weighed in at 10lb 9oz, and I'm jumping for joy – and the other fellow was going as mad as me, he had never seen a tench like it.

I popped her in a sack and returned to bed, but sleep did not come easily, since my mind was racing with the night's events. Warren Hammond came down in the morning and took the photos, and before he left I managed another of 8lb 10oz. I packed up at about 11am. I phoned Jim Cheverall with the news, and managed to persuade him to join me the following night for a three-day session. He had only been out once this season after having his best season ever the year before.

We arrived mid-afternoon, and thankfully the swims were empty. It was warm and overcast, with the occasional sunny spell as we bombarded the swims with groundbait. By the time we had the rods out it was 5.30pm; it was nice to have some company, besides the prospect of catching a few good fish.

At 7.20pm I opened my account with a 6lb 11oz male, followed thirty minutes later by a small carp. Then twenty minutes

July 2000: this weighed in at 10lb 9oz and I was literally jumping for joy.

later Jim had his first tench of the season, a fine specimen of 8lb 5oz. We chatted a while longer, and then retired to bed since we wanted to be up early in the morning.

I slept through until the alarm clock went off at 5am; Jim had taken an 8lb 1oz tench at about 2am and had decided to stay up. A few tench rolled at dawn over our spots, but no action was forthcoming, even though we re-cast regularly. Breakfast was late as usual, and just as typically my

near-in rod screamed off half way through cooking it. The fish just plodded about as I slowly edged her towards the bank; Jim netted her first time, and soon we were looking at another monster tench on the unhooking mat. Jim did the honours with the weighing, and a weight of 10lb 6oz was given. I couldn't believe it: was the magic of Papercourt ever going to end?

As the day unfolded my swim remained quiet, until three six-pounders graced my net in the early evening. Jim had been busy landing five tench, the best two going 8lb 11oz and 8lb 15oz. Two very happy anglers sat there that evening, as a constant stream of visitors popped into the swim wanting to know how all the fish were being caught. Strangely enough, although we told them the truth, I felt many didn't believe it could be that simple.

The following day the fish fed early and continued until 9.30am, then again in the early evening when the heat from the baking sun started to ease off. Jim managed three tench, the best 8lb 15oz, whilst I continued my run of good fortune, landing five tench that included specimens of 8lb 14oz, 8lb 15oz and the black one down in weight at 9lb 11oz.

The night was cold and clear, with a heavy mist at dawn: it was going to be another scorcher of a day. I had the only run at 9.20am from a 7lb 3oz tench, and then the heat finally beat us; we packed away at 11.30am, stopping off for a celebratory pint on the way home.

The hot weather stayed and the tench spawned, putting an end to the fishing for a year – but what a year! I have never caught so many big tench from a water in a season before or since, and in view of the fact that I only did four short sessions makes it even more incredible. Thank you, Papercourt, for some of the best fishing of my life.

RETURN TO FERRIS

I began the spring of 2001 on a local 80-acre pit along with my son David. We had done a couple of two-day trips accounting for nearly thirty tench, the best of 8lb 14oz to the young lad, when news reached me that Ferris Meadow had changed hands. Knowing that it had produced many quality fish the season before, I had longed to return for some time, and was soon signing

on for the season, along with a few other expectant anglers.

Unfortunately we couldn't make a start as we had planned, because over the winter the Thames had been spilling into the pit for the best part of three months, and the water was still up by four feet in April, with most of the swims underwater. We dug a drainage ditch to let the water run back into the river, which was now trickling past at its normal level, but by May when the fishing began, the water was still up two feet, so that most swims were only fishable in boots or waders.

My friend Warren Hammond and I decided to target a hotspot known as the 'Pier', with Warren doing extended weekends and myself weekdays. He had the first few days with no action, then I followed suit. The pit had appeared lifeless throughout our sessions and after another blank session each, we started to wonder if all the extra water had kept the water temperature down, slowing the tench's metabolism. There was also a strange lack of weed.

We decided that a move to warmer, shallower water might pay off, so we opted for two swims on the opposite bank. I moved into a corner swim where the fish usually spawn, which offered depths of four feet on a large plateau next to the island, while Warren tried the 'Beach', which gently shelves and also has access to the shallowest end of a large bar 100 yards out, and normally only three feet deep.

Again there was no action, and no one else caught either; but on the last morning of my stay I saw a lot of tench rolling, working their way down the main bar towards Warren. He still had a couple of days to go, so I wished him luck and arranged to move in when he left, as I was due some holiday.

The following morning I received a few text messages from Wol, describing how the action had started: he had taken four tench including females of 10lb 8oz and 9lb, plus an 8lb male. With another two days to wait I was itching to get down there, but the following day brought no news of further action.

The next morning after finishing my night shift, I was outside the tackle shop for opening time, eager to be at Ferris. With plenty of fresh casters and maggots and a couple of bags of Richworth strawberry jam mini boilies purchased, I hastily drove the four miles to the pit. After barrowing my gear round to the 'Beach', I discovered Wol had not had any action, though he had seen a few fish roll near his bait.

The best part of the day was spent setting up camp and inspecting what could be seen of the lake bed from the dinghy; everywhere I could see was covered in a dark silty deposit left by the floodwater. With no evidence of any feeding spots, I decided to position two rods on the shallowest point of the main bar, then placed the other two on to different small bars within casting range, hoping that the tops of the bars would have least debris on them. All areas were baited with a mixture of brown crumb, hemp, wheat, casters and a few mini boilies, using the dinghy to keep the bait as tight as possible. The two rods that were being cast, were initially lowered on to the spots before tying on the marker knots.

The first two nights and days were biteless, although the fish betrayed their presence at dawn each morning, rolling in the vicinity of my long-range marker floats. With the dinghy revealing no real feeding spots within my swim, I had established an approach of carefully studying the position of the rolling fish in comparison to the floats (no mean feat at 100 yards, even with binoculars), then repositioning the floats behind the spots.

After another uneventful night I was up at first light eager to watch the pit unwind

its secrets. As the horizon glowed red, odd swirls could be seen in the vicinity of my distant markers, and as the light strengthened, I could distinguish the culprits as tench, and, even better, they appeared to be right over my left spot.

Not until 6.30am did the 2oz bobbin drop 2in, followed by a steady pull of the bait runner – and my first tench was on. It plodded about as I slowly pumped it towards the bank, my legs like jelly as my mind visualized the yet unseen monster – when suddenly, thirty yards out, the hook pulled out. I was numb! It had taken casters on the bottom hook, and although the hook appeared faultless I tied on a fresh one, and once I had regained my composure a little, I rowed out and repositioned my rig.

At 11.30am I pulled out of another tench on the same rod, this time a male of 5–6lb, followed at 5.30pm with a similar occurrence by a female of about 7lb. By this time I was devastated; all three fish had taken casters on the bottom hook, on rigs I had caught countless tench on with only minimal hook pulls. I guessed the tench were still not feeding over-confidently, so decided to give them a bit more rope to hang themselves on. I extended the hooklengths from 4in to 9in, and replaced the size 10T6 Raptor with a lighter Super Specialist.

Dawn was quiet on day four, with only one tench spotted rolling close to one of my near-in rods; hopefully a bite would be forthcoming from the area sooner or later. I have lost count, over the years, of the times I have had a tench occasionally roll over my bait for two or three days, then I catch it and the rolling stops, and the spot ceases to produce any further action.

A steady drop-back at 11.30am brought me down to earth, and as I connected, a heavy headshaking sensation pulsated down the rod. I steadily gained line, and then seventy yards out a large flank broke surface as what I could now see was a large bream begrudgingly came towards the bank. At 13lb 2oz I was well pleased; it was a beautiful long, dark male, and again it had taken casters off the same spot.

Day five passed uneventfully, and it was not until 5am on day six, my final day, when the same rod gave me a new personal best bream of 14lb 2oz, another long, dark male.

With no action forthcoming on my right rod, fishing a mere four yards down the same bar, I repositioned both rigs six feet apart in the hot area, and prayed I wouldn't get too many crossed lines if I hooked anything. At 12.05pm a 6lb 8oz male picked up the casters on the newly positioned rig, followed by one of 8lb 15oz at 12.30 pm, on double boilies to the same rod. Unfortunately my six days were over, and I now had to vacate the pit for twenty-four hours, as laid down in the rules, knowing for certain the swim would be taken on my return.

After spending a night at home, I decided I would probably revisit the 80-acre pit I had started the spring on, as young David was accompanying me for the final two nights of my holiday. I thought he could catch some more tench, but he insisted he wanted to go to Ferris and spin for the pike.

As we pulled into the car park two unknown cars were present, but as I looked across the pit, I could see my swim was vacant. The minimal amount of tackle was hurried round in sheer panic to secure the swim, expecting at any moment to find another angler leap from the bushes ahead of me.

With the swim now secured and adrenalin levels lowered, I set about retrieving the rest of the tackle mountain from the car. I was all sorted by mid-afternoon, and had rebaited my spots from the dinghy. This time I only put loosefeed over the long-range spot, having decided to fish 'time-bomb' style (this involves moulding a tennis size ball of groundbait around an inline lead) to make the hookbait area more attractive, as bites had been few and far between.

I decided to leave the swim in peace until dusk, when I would row my rigs out, hopefully allowing the fish to feed confidently. The afternoon was spent as a pike ghillie, netting and unhooking half-a-dozen pike to nearly 12lb, in between brewing up for any visitors.

By evening Warren had reappeared and went in the 'Pier' swim for a couple of nights, and Rory and Jackie set up near him, then came round for a chat. We talked as only anglers can, of what might be, what size tench were out there, why was it so hard this year, and where was all the weed?

At 11.15pm I had a steady drop-back on one of my long-range rods, and hooked a tench that immediately took a few yards of line. At that range I knew it was a good fish, and it seemed like forever before it swirled twenty yards out. Thankfully its spirit was gone, and I soon had her within netting range, only to find she had become tethered in the mini pads that grew out some four yards from the bank. Each time I pushed the net towards her she moved further away, and all I could see were my two red boilies hanging from her large open mouth. Desperately I filled my waders, and eventually she was mine.

As we unwrapped her from the mesh I knew she was well over 10lb, and as the needle settled right on 11lb I was elated: my biggest Ferris tench. After sacking her in some deeper margins I dropped my rig back off and sat there buzzing. We chatted some more, and there was crazy talk of a brace of 11lb-plus tench. Eventually the others returned to their own swims and I

June 2002: Ferris Meadows' final 'double' – 10lb 13oz.

slept fitfully, re-living the moments of the capture – that is, until I was dragged from my pit at 5am by a small male that fell off near the net.

At 7am a run on one of the near-in rods resulted in a 7lb 1oz male, again on a boilie (my solitary roller). This was the cue for everyone to start assembling for the photo session, and as usual demands for mugs of tea, prior to the event.

Unbelievably, just after 8am when everyone was assembled, one of the long-range rods ripped off, and as fifteen yards from the clutch swiftly followed, it was thought that one of the rare carp that inhabit the pit was the culprit. The lads removed my other rods from the swim, as the carp started to feel more and more like a big tench; by this time my nerve was deteriorating rapidly. Eventually the fish could be seen kiting left, about twenty yards out just under the surface; everyone agreed it looked enormous. Then it turned and headed back out, taking twenty yards of line off the clutch.

'Why is it going the wrong way?' I shouted, as everyone laughed at my trembling legs. Slowly but surely I regained line, praying my hook would hold. This time she appeared ten yards out, and finally allowed herself to be drawn to my waiting net; then I stood there for a moment or two as panic turned to euphoria.

On the mat she looked huge, definitely over 11lb, and some predicted over 12lb; I couldn't watch as Chris put her on the Avons. The official reading was 11lb 8oz, and a new personal best: I was in a daze. The lads sacked her up for ten minutes while I recovered, then photos were taken of both fish and they were returned.

Everyone hung around for a while, and after re-rowing my baits, I promptly caught a 3½lb male, which we all found quite amusing. I was to leave the following morning, and Rory was going in behind me, hoping to catch a good fish or two.

On the final morning I had a 6lb female at 5.30am, a nice fish to end the session with. It's always hard to pack up, as I am always thinking that the next giant could be minutes away from being on my hook. It's even harder when you know the swim will be gone for the foreseeable future.

It was a full seventeen days before I returned to Ferris, and in that period not a lot had been caught. Rory had taken a 9lb 14oz tench from the 'Beach', along with a smaller one, and had lost a big one on a hook pull; now Dave Ball was in the swim for three days, and as I sat and chatted to him I pondered where to fish. Nothing had been caught from more than 8ft of water, yet a deep-water swim on the opposite bank kept calling me.

Eventually I gave in to it, and by 7.45pm had three rigs positioned at varying distances from the bank; around each was placed a dozen tangerine-sized balls of brown crumb, laced with hemp, wheat and casters. I didn't go mad on the bait as I was only expecting to ambush passing fish.

I couldn't believe it when at 8.30pm, as I was watching Dave ball-playing a fish from his boat, my inside rod in sixteen feet of water ripped off. After a good battle, with a few anxious moments when netting it between my other lines, another double-figure tench was on my unhooking mat. At 10lb 9oz it was one of the best conditioned big tench I had ever seen, and thankfully Jackie Davis turned up just afterwards, so he did the honours with the camera.

Dave's tench turned out to be a little over 7lb, which he quickly followed up with a similar-sized specimen. Unfortunately this seemed to spell the end of the action for the season, with nothing caught over the next month. Rory stayed on alone, and at the end of August got his reward with a 10lb 13oz beast.

If we thought the fishing had been hard that year, little did we know how it was to

August 2001: Rory saw it through to the bitter end, and was rewarded with his 10lb 13oz August giant.

develop. The 2002 season started slow and stayed there, with a grand total of twelve tench being landed. Fortunately I had the only double at 10lb 13oz, with Rory taking the only other tench of note at 9lb 3oz.

With only four out of twenty-five members catching anything the previous year, the 2003 season began with only eighteen tickets sold. This year was to be the cruellest of all, yielding a grand total of five tench caught, the best one being 8lb 14oz, my first one out. Rory had two tench and I had the other three. Even more depressing, three out of the five captures were the same fish, and to make matters worse, about a

hundred 4lb to 8lb bream had come in from the Thames during the winter floods, and were proving to be a serious nuisance once they found your baited spots.

Sadly for me this heralded the end of Ferris Meadow, a water where dreams came true for many. It had its highs and lows, but it was always magical and mysterious, always leaving you wondering what secrets lay unlocked within its depths. Its peace and tranquillity are second to none, making it the sort of place you become a part of. The fishing becomes secondary, and just being there is privilege enough. Total escapism!

UK Top 50 Tench
As of 26 May 2005

	Weight	Notes	Captor	Location	Month	Year
1	15.03.06	(1)	Darren Ward	Southern stillwater	June	2001
2	14.08.00		Karl Connolly	Fishers Green	Oct	2004
3	14.08.00	(2)	Gordan Bevan	Herts lake	Sept	1993
4	14.04.00		Gary Newman	Bury Lake	Aug	1994
5	14.03.00	(2)	Phil Gooriah	Wraysbury 1	June	1987
6	14.00.00		Gordan Bevan	Herts lake	Sept	1993
7	14.00.00		Alan Wilson	Wilstone Res.	June	1992
8	13.07.00		Gary Newman	Bury Lake	Sept	1994
9	13.05.00		John Scott	Woodpecker Pool	May	2004
10	13.05.00		Paul Woodford	Tring	June	1998
11	12.15.00		Gary Newman	Bury Lake	Sept	1994
12	12.13.00		Dean Franklin	Wilstone Res.	Sept	1995
13	12.12.00		Carl Street	Sywell Res.	Nov	2003
14	12.08.11	(2)	Alan Wilson	Wilstone Res.	June	1985
15	12.08.00		Michael French	Southern stillwater	Aug	2003
16	12.08.00		Nick Cooke	Wilstone Res.	Oct	1995
17	12.08.00		Cathy McCorkell	Startops Res.	June	1990
18	12.08.00	(3)	R. Blaber	R. Kennet	Feb	1951
19	12.08.00		Pam???	Startops Res.	???	???
20	12.07.00		Oliver Moore	Tring	June	1998
21	12.07.00		Rick Seal	R. Avon (Bristol)	Dec	1998
22	12.06.00		Dave Ball	Korda Fishery	June	2004
23	12.06.00		Alan Wilson	Wilstone Res.	June	1993
24	12.05.08		Peter Pope	Private lake Wraysbury	June	1999
25	12.04.00		Ross McLintock	Berkshire stillwater	June	2004
26	12.03.00		Martin Thorpe	Hampshire stillwater	July	2004
27	12.03.00		Dave Ball	Korda Fishery	July	2004
28	12.01.08		Phil Martyn	Half Pit	June	2001

UK Top 50 Tench
As of 26 May 2005

	Weight	Notes	Captor	Location	Month	Year
29	12.01.00		Andy Smith	Surry gravel pit	June	2002
30	12.00.08		Rory Adair	Surrey lake	July	1995
31	12.00.00		Paul Martin	Korda Fishery	Sept	2004
32	12.00.00		Michael Baldwin	Essex gravel pit	June	2004
33	12.00.00		Marcus Powell	Linear Fisheries	June	2004
34	12.00.00		Neil Berry	Horseshoe Lake	July	2002
35	11.15.00		Jim Eggleton	Half Pit	June	2001
36	11.14.00		Matt Skelly	Rackerhayes	July	2001
37	11.13.00		Dave Ball	Korda Fishery	June	2004
38	11.12.00		Neil Berry	Horseshoe Lake	July	2002
39	11.12.00		Jim Eldridge	Essex lake	June	1997
40	11.11.00		Andy Nellist	Wilstone Res.	June	2003
41	11.11.00		Tony Miles	Midlands stillwater	June	1999
42	11.10.00		Paul Iafrati	Colne Valley Pit	July	2004
43	11.10.00		Dave Ball	Korda Fishery	June	2004
44	11.10.00		Jim Wells	Newbury gravel pit	June	2002
45	11.10.00		Mick Stevens	Midlands stillwater	June	2002
46	11.10.00		Roy Woodford	Wilstone Res.	June	1993
47	11.10.00		Bob Henderson	Wilstone Res.	June	1991
48	11.09.00		Chris Turbull	Midlands stillwater	June	2003
49	11.09.00		Dave Green	Northfield Half Pit	June	1999
50	11.08.00		Chris Stothard	Surrey lake	July	1994

Notes
1. Current British Record; 2. Previous British Record; 3. Not accepted due to 'abnormal condition'

The above top 50 tench list was submitted by Graham Bailey of The Tenchfishers; we thank Graham and the club for their kind interest.

Index